"I learned the hard way that an author must have at least a basic understanding of what copyright is and how to protect it in this global society. Thankfully, *Copyright Companion for Writers* covers everything writers should know about copyright, fair use and public domain, plagiarism, international copyright issues, and the industry's hot topics that affect writers. And amazingly, Tonya Evans-Walls presents the information in a reader-friendly way that is easy to understand and digest. The forms on CD-ROM and the glossary are a definite plus! This book is an essential reference that no writer should be without."

—*Brian Jud, author of* Beyond the Bookstore

"Finally, a book that answers many of the questions and resolves some of the major misconceptions we hear about copyright every day. This will save independent authors and publishers a lot of heartache—and a lot of money!"

—*Jim Barnes, Independent Publisher Online*

"At almost every writing workshop I run, the question about registering copyright comes up, and I am always embarrassed that I don't know how to respond. Now I can confidently reply, 'Read chapter 3 of *Copyright Companion for Writers.*' But don't stop there. Go back and start at the beginning of the book because having a thorough working knowledge of your rights is vital to your success as a writer. If, like me, you're usually overwhelmed and intimidated by legalese, don't worry. Tonya makes it all amazingly easy to understand and uses examples from current news items to drive home important points. *Copyright Companion for Writers* is a must-have for every writer's library."

—*Bonnie Neubauer, author of* Write-Brain Workbook: 366 Exercises to Liberate Your Writing, *and inventor of Story Spinner, www. BonnieNeubauer.com*

Copyright Companion for Writers

Tonya M. Evans-Walls

Legal Write Publications

Imprint of FYOS Entertainment, LLC

Philadelphia

Printed in the United States of America

Published 2007

14 13 12 11 10 09 08 07   1 2 3 4 5

ISBN-13: 978-0-9674579-9-4

ISBN-10: 0-9674579-9-8

Publisher's Cataloging-in-Publication

(Provided by Quality Books, Inc.)

       Evans, Tonya Marie.
           Copyright companion for writers / Tonya M.
       Evans-Walls ; foreword by Dan Poynter.
           p. cm. -- (Literary entrepreneur series)
           Includes index.
           ISBN-13: 978-0-9674579-9-4
           ISBN-10: 0-9674579-9-8

           1. Authors -- Legal status, laws, etc. -- United States --
       Popular works. 2. Copyright -- United States -- Popular
       works.   I. Title. II. Series.

       KF390.A96E925 2006   346.7304'82
           QBI06-600269

Request for permissions to reproduce any portion of this book should be addressed to

Legal Write Publications

ATTN: Permissions Department

P.O. Box 25216

Philadelphia, PA 19119

Or to info@legalwritepublications.com

LE Series™ Books and logo, the Legal Write Publications logo, and the title and trade dress of the *Copyright Companion for Writers* are the intellectual property of Legal Write Publications.

Editing by Lisa A. Smith, www.writing-at-work.com

Interior design by Deb Tremper, www.sixpennygraphics.com

Cover design by James Jones

Visit the publisher's Web site at www.legalwritepublications.com.

To the light of my life, my husband, Orville Russel Walls, III; and to God, with thanks for the opportunity to use my gifts to help others pursue their passion for writing and publishing

DISCLAIMER

Contents

Foreword

Since meeting Tonya in the small press area at the 2001 BookExpo America in Chicago, Illinois, I have enjoyed watching her publishing company and her Literary Entrepreneur Series grow into a successful endeavor that, like my company, Para Publishing, is dedicated to encouraging and educating writers to become informed and successful published authors.

The *Literary Law Guide for Authors*, the first in the Literary Entrepreneur Series, contains information desperately needed by authors and publishers alike about copyright, trademark, and contracts. And it's all presented in an informative and entertaining way, which is no small feat when dealing with such complex legal issues. This second book in the series, *Copyright Companion for Writers*, focuses just on copyright. As a result, topics like fair use, public domain, international copyright issues, transferring and reclaiming copyright, electronic rights, and locating copyright owners for permissions are covered more completely and in greater depth.

In this digital age, copyright law is ever changing. Fortunately, Tonya researches the topics covered in her books up to the moment before they actually go to print, thereby ensuring that each one has the most up-to-date legal information available. For instance, this book contains the July 1, 2006, change in the copyright registration fee. Her commitment to accurate and timely information is one of the many things that make Tonya's series of legal reference guides for writers and industry professionals so significant.

Whether you are a new writer or an experienced and published author, in *Copyright Companion for Writers* you will find helpful information about the nature of copyright; how it is created, protected, and licensed; and how new technologies affect copyright creation and protection. The book also covers hot topics like Google Print, the Freelancer Settlement case, and the orphan-works debate, and even gives important information every freelancer and songwriter should know.

This book has everything a writer needs to know about copyright and more. You will undoubtedly refer to the *Copyright Companion for Writers* at every phase of the writing and publishing process. From the first chapter to the valuable forms contained in the appendix and on the companion CD-ROM, each section addresses your most basic and pressing questions in a way that you will easily understand. Tonya makes it possible for you to quickly learn what you need to know about publishing law and intellectual property. I do not know of another book that covers all of these topics in such a complete, down-to-earth, and understandable fashion, and I highly recommend it for every writer's reference shelf.

Copyright Companion for Writers is a well-written, essential guide for those who are serious about understanding their rights and avoiding the legal pitfalls of writing and publishing in the twenty-first century. I strongly believe that you cannot be a successful author and publisher without effectively examining the law as it relates to the publishing industry.

Dan Poynter, *The Self-Publishing Manual*

Preface

A legal reference guide is only as good as the timeliness and relevance of the information it contains. This is particularly true in the case of copyright law because each year new court rulings and legislative amendments emerge to address the technological and other advances that make it both easier and more challenging for writers to publish and to protect their work, and to make a living in the process.

This first edition of *Copyright Companion for Writers* is the second of the LE Series Books™ for literary entrepreneurs. In this first edition, I build on the chapters devoted to copyright law in my book *Literary Law Guide for Authors: Copyright, Trademark, and Contracts in Plain Language*, and update, revise, and expand the information for a more comprehensive survey of copyright law so that writers can understand more fully their rights and responsibilities and can maximize the value of their work.

This first edition provides information on

- electronic rights
- reclaiming your copyright
- why and when you should register your copyright
- the difference between fair use and public domain
- when a work enters the public domain
- international copyright issues
- legalities of writing about real people and events
- the most recent cases and controversies in copyright law
- pending and recent legislation affecting writers
- information that every freelancer should know
- information that every songwriter should know

This first edition also provides a glossary, an appendix of important forms such as the one for copyright registration, and an accompanying CD-ROM that contains those forms as PDF files.

This legal reference guide will help you to increase your knowledge about your intellectual property and your contractual rights as a writer, and help you learn more about how to use other people's words and other copyrighted works legally in your own work; it will also guide you in dispelling myths like the Poor Man's Copyright. After reading this book, freelancers should also better understand how to protect and increase the value of their electronic rights in the twenty-first century. This book, and its sister publication, *Contracts Companion for Writers*, are the perfect partners for you to take with you on your creative journey to literary success.

Symbol Key

When you see this symbol . . .   **It means . . .**

 Myth: Presents, examines, and dispels a common myth.

 Note: Draws your attention to a particular topic of interest.

 Question: Presents and answers a frequently asked question.

 Checklist: Lists several items to consider on a particular topic.

 Legal Note: Examines the facts and disposition of a leading case, or the status of a statute or pending legislation.

 Form: Provides the applicable form in Appendix B and on the accompanying CD-ROM.

1 What Copyright Is and Why You Should Care

No one word is more misused or more misunderstood by writers than the word "copyright." This single word creates such confusion and lends itself to so much misinformation because rumors, assumptions, and complicated changes in the law make it difficult for writers to separate fact from fiction. But because copyright consists of such a valuable bundle of rights, it is imperative that writers fully comprehend the nature of copyright and the process by which it is protected.

Writers are not the only ones confused by the word "copyright." More than a few business-savvy agents, publishers, and even attorneys, who are in the business of negotiating rights, have a woefully inadequate understanding of the nature of copyright. This is particularly troublesome because of the way the publishing industry is set up for traditional publishing through the major New York publishing houses. Agents and legal professionals are the gatekeepers between writers and publishers, providing writers with access to the editorial decision-makers and providing publishers with a steady stream of available literary properties. Thus, writers often—and unquestioningly—trust these industry professionals to protect their interests. But the explanation that "it's always done this way" is simply not good enough when valuable rights are at stake. And although you may very well not understand all of the legal intricacies of copyright, for you to successfully protect your copyrights and to enjoy potentially lucrative financial benefits from successful negotiations to license and sell your rights, you must first understand how copyright is created and protected.

You need to know

- what questions to ask
- what the potential pitfalls may be
- how your interests and those of your agent may be similar from a financial perspective (get as much money as possible!) but different in many other important respects (when rights revert, when you get paid, what types of sales and payment reports you get, who

1

gets your subsidiary rights such as electronic and foreign rights—
and the list goes on)

You should also understand and appreciate the differences between the various types of intellectual property, and you should know how new technologies affect your legal rights and responsibilities in the digital age and beyond.

Copyright is a type of intellectual property that relates to and governs a primary means—artistic and literary—by which our cultural and historical identity is developed, cultivated, and preserved. Intellectual property has been defined generally as "creations of the mind" that are afforded the status of property and thus have value that is capable of protection. Intellectual property is governed by various national and international laws, and generally gives its owner the exclusive right to do or authorize certain things regarding the property. Copyright is just one of a number of different types of intellectual property.

The Name Game: Copyright, Trademark, or Patent?

What you don't know about intellectual property ownership can jeopardize your rights and potentially expose you to legal liability. So let's take a closer look at the differences between the various types of intellectual property.

Copyright: A copyright protects an author's original artistic or literary work, whether published or unpublished. Under copyright law, the term "author" has a special meaning: the creator of an original literary or artistic work. Thus, the word "author" applies not only to writers but to photographers, singers, painters, sculptors—anyone who creates a literary or artistic work. Examples of literary and artistic works include manuscripts, book covers, song lyrics, sheet music, musical scores, paintings, sketches, sound recordings (music), films, and photographs. And those lists are not all-inclusive.

Trademark: A trademark protects a word, phrase, symbol, or device—the mark—used in business (referred to in the law as commerce) to identify and distinguish one product from another. For example, Jump at the Sun® is a registered trademark for children's fiction and nonfiction books about history, sports, the arts, spirituality, musicians, biography, friendship, family, poetry, and school.

Service Mark: A service mark protects a word, phrase, symbol, or device—again, the mark—used in business to identify and distinguish one service from another. For example, Lightning Source® is a registered service mark for wholesale distributorship services in the field of on-demand printing and electronic media.

Patent: The patent is probably the least used intellectual property in the publishing industry. A patent protects an invention by granting the inventor the right to exclude others from producing or using the inventor's discovery or invention for a specific period of time. Some examples of patentable inventions include the talking book, an e-book reader, a typewriter, and an Internet-based system and method for highlighting search results such as that used by Google. Not all intellectual property lawyers practice patent law because a patent practice requires that attorneys have a science degree and take an additional bar examination; patent attorneys usually have some background in technology or engineering.

Plagiarism or Infringement?

Dictionary.com defines plagiarism as "a piece of writing that has been copied from someone else and is presented as being your own work," or "taking someone's words or ideas as if they were your own." We're all familiar with the concept from high school or college. A paper or project is due at 9:00 a.m. on Monday; but at 9:00 p.m. the night before, the student has barely typed the first word. Panic sets in and, perhaps, situational ethics takes hold. Whether overwhelmed, imprecise, or just plain lazy, the student takes a bit from here and a bit from there, and soon a finished product appears—one whose words or thoughts are not 100 percent original—and the student presents it as his or her own work. That's plagiarism.

But plagiarism is not just for pimple-faced students anymore. It's gone high tech now. I am sure countless high-powered execs and law partners have presented the words of someone else as their own. And let's not forget the many scandals involving journalists, which seems to me even more onerous since, at least in theory, a journalist's entire profession rests on intellectual honesty in writing and reporting about our world. There was the infamous *New York Times* scandal involving the writer Jayson Blair; other problems at that paper involving Charlie LeDuff and Bernard Weinraub; Jack Kelley, who resigned from *USA Today*—the list goes on and on.

And it's never been easier to find and copy information on any topic because it's available online 24 hours a day, 7 days a week, 365 days a year. It has also never been easier to hide intellectual theft. The Internet has provided access to innumerable bits of information that can be cut and pasted into a word document and claimed as one's own. And the vast breadth of this information can make it pretty difficult to ferret out the dreaded plagiarizers.

Plagiarism is a white-hot industry, too, especially for those who promote and sell information to those who are willing to pay top dollar to avoid having to do the work themselves. A simple Internet search yielded more than 418,000,000—yes, 418,000,000—hits for term papers available online. Thankfully, a war on plagiarism has been waged by organizations like Plagiarism.org and sites like Turnitin.com, which compares text against millions of documents available on the Internet and against a database of some fifteen million other documents to counteract instances of this plague on education.

Of course, plagiarism plagues the book-publishing industry too. In June 2006, I released a podcast about one such ugly incident: KaavyaGate. Kaavya Viswanathan, who was an undergraduate enrolled in Harvard at the time, signed a big-time six-figure publishing deal with Little, Brown and Company for her book *How Opal Mehta Got Kissed, Got Wild, and Got a Life*. Little, Brown published the book in April 2006, and soon pulled it from the shelves amid a plagiarism scandal uncovered by Harvard's school paper, the *Harvard Crimson*.

Initial reports found that passages in Viswanathan's book bore a striking resemblance to various passages in two books written by Megan McCafferty. In fact, the paper reported that one fourteen-word passage from McCafferty's book *Sloppy Firsts* appeared word-for-word in Viswanathan's book. The paper detailed other passages that were almost exactly the same in the two authors' works and posted the information on its Web site.

As if that weren't enough, the *New York Times* conducted its own investigation and uncovered yet a third instance of plagiarism with several instances of character descriptions, concepts, and plot lines that were almost the same in Viswanathan's book and in *Can You Keep a Secret?* by Sophie Kinsella, instances that were too similar to be coincidental. And an investigation by the *Boston Globe* discovered that Viswanathan's book showed even more instances of plagiarism from Meg Cabot's book *The Princess Diaries*.

What was Viswanathan's explanation? Well, in the case of McCafferty's work, Viswanathan called it "internalizing" McCafferty's voice. But nearly everyone else, including the publisher, called it plagiarism; and I suspect the publisher wants its $500K advance back. DreamWorks, which had optioned the film rights to the book, dropped the project as well.

This likely will be a hard—and expensive—lesson learned for what appears to be one of the most egregious instances of plagiarism we've seen recently—Jayson Blair notwithstanding. Expensive not just in terms of money but also in reputation, honor, and pride. I think intellectual integrity is important. Words have power and should be used properly to communicate, to empower, and to inform, not to "get over" and "make a buck."

Now, some people are confused about the difference between plagiarism and copyright infringement. Think of it this way: All plagiarism is infringement, but not all infringement is plagiarism. The reason is that copyright owners hold a bundle of rights (as discussed in chapter 2). Copyright owners have the right to copy, distribute, make derivative works from, perform, and display their work; and to allow or prevent others from doing so regardless of whether proper attribution is given. And, contrary to popular belief, there is no set number of words that can be used without permission. So if you are using someone else's copyrighted work in your own, and no fair use exception applies, you should seek permission—not just properly attribute the work to the owner. Attribution is a good start, but by itself it's not enough to avoid infringement.

So someone can actually copy another's work, say "I've copied this from Patsi Pen," and still be liable for copyright infringement—again, depending on the fair use analysis and assuming the work is not in the public domain. But plagiarizers don't even bother to properly attribute the borrowed text. They simply claim that all ideas and thoughts as expressed on the page (or computer screen) are original. Even if the plagiarizers do not actually state that they are expressing original ideas in a literary work, the lack of such statements does not remove the taint of plagiarism.

The Value of Intellectual Property

Over the last decade, a number of studies about the value of intellectual property have estimated that more than 50 percent of U.S. exports relate to or depend on some form of intellectual property protection. Fifty years ago, the number was closer to 10 percent. Additionally, *Copyright Industries in the U.S. Economy: The 2004 Report*, prepared by Stephen E. Siwak for the International Intellectual Property Alliance, states that the value added to the U.S. economy by "core" copyright industries (for example, newspapers, book publishing, recording, music, periodicals, motion pictures, radio and TV broadcasts, software) reached $626.2 billion or 6 percent of the U.S. economy in 2002. The value added by the total copyright industries was $1.254 trillion or 12 percent of the U.S. economy. Further, the core copyright industries employed 4.02 percent of U.S. workers in 2002 (roughly the same percentage as those employed in the U.S. construction industry). Unfortunately, foreign sales were not as impressive, and all major segments within the entertainment and news industries experienced declines in their foreign sales revenues in 2002, except for the motion picture segment, which experienced an increase, reaching $17 billion in foreign sales revenue for that year. But overall, the economic benefits to the United States from intellectual property are impressive.

Apart from their economic benefits to society, literary and artistic contributions have proven to be an integral part of individual, community, and societal success—and these benefits are the true cornerstone of the overall benefits of intellectual creativity to society as a whole. Thus, intellectual property remains as important in today's society as it was when the drafters gathered to create the constitutional right of an author to control the use of his or her writings, art, or discoveries. This right is deeply rooted in American law. As stated in the U.S. Constitution, article I, section 8:

> The Congress shall have Power . . . To promote the Progress of Science and useful Arts, by securing for limited Times to Authors and Inventors the exclusive Right to their respective Writings and Discoveries.

Copyright and trademark laws are of particular interest and concern to writers because they relate integrally to the writing process.

A Brief History of Copyright Law

The first national bill to establish copyright law in the United States was passed by Congress in 1790 and signed into law by George Washington on May 31, 1790. The purpose of this law was "for the encouragement of learning, by securing the copies of maps, Charts, And [sic] books, to the authors and proprietors of such copies, during the times therein mentioned." The duration of copyright at that time was fourteen years from date of registration, with an additional fourteen-year extension if renewed. Congress has since made several substantial revisions to the law.

Act of 1909

The first major revision occurred in 1909 and was codified in 1947 as Title 17 of the Copyright Act. The 1909 act required strict adherence to the formalities of copyright notice, registration, and renewal. Therefore, works that were otherwise protectable could fall into the public domain if any of the formalities were not satisfied. The 1909 act continues to apply to works created before January 1, 1978. Note that care should be taken if a new work, otherwise governed by the Revised Act of 1976, incorporates parts of a prior work that is governed by the 1909 act.

Act of 1976

The 1909 act was substantially revised in 1976. This first version of the 1976 act (see page 7 for the revised version)—also commonly referred to by writers and publishers as the Act of 1989—applies to works created between January 1, 1978, and February 28, 1989; those years are known as the Decennial Era of Copyright Law. While somewhat less stringent than the 1909 law, the 1976 act still required authors to adhere to certain formalities of notice and registration, and denied copyright protection for any works that failed to comply, moving them into the public domain.

Revised Act of 1976

In 1989, Congress revised the 1976 act to amend certain provisions so that United States copyright law would comply with the Berne Convention for the Protection of Literary and Artistic Works. The Berne Convention is an international copyright treaty that requires all signatories to eliminate the requirements for notice and registration as a condition of copyright protection. Formalities like notice and registration are still important, however, because works created after 1978 and before 1989 are governed by the original version of the 1976 act. As of this writing, 161 countries are signed to the Berne Convention.

One of the most prominent and important concepts recognized and protected by the Berne Convention is the concept of moral rights. The term "moral rights" (or *droit moral*) encompasses the right of attribution and the right of integrity. The right of attribution ensures that artists are properly identified with the works they create and are not associated with works they did not create. The right of integrity prevents the intentional distortion, mutilation, or other modification of a work of art that injures an artist's honor or reputation.

Moral rights are personal to the author and therefore may not be transferred to another person. Moral rights may be waived, however, by a written document signed by the author. Moral rights have been recognized for many years by most European countries and by other signatory nations of the Berne Convention, but not explicitly by the United States.

When Congress amended the 1976 act, it expressly declared that the Berne Convention protections are not self-executing (not automatically incorporated by reference into U.S. law), that claims arising under the Berne Convention must be handled according to the existing laws of the United States, and that no further rights beyond those expressly included by amendment are recognized. The practical effect of these declarations was that Congress declined to adopt the moral rights provisions of the Berne Convention, stating that the rights of attribution and integrity were sufficiently protected under existing federal, state, and local laws. That conclusion was challenged and ultimately addressed, in part, in 1990.

Visual Arts Rights Act of 1990

Realizing the inconsistency between United States copyright law and the Berne Convention in regard to moral rights, Congress enacted the Visual Arts Rights Act (VARA) to grant visual artists, such as painters and sculptors, the rights of attribution and integrity for certain one-of-a-kind and limited-edition prints of visual art works.

 In the 2001 case *Flack v. Friends of Queen Catherine, Inc.*, the federal district court in the Southern District of New York held that a grossly negligent or intentional modification of a work of visual art may be actionable under VARA.

The passage of VARA was the first instance in which the United States recognized and expressly granted moral rights, but Congress did so in a very limited way. VARA extended moral rights protection to visual artists who create paintings, drawings, limited prints, sculptures, and still photographs produced for exhibition purposes only. The Copyright Act enumerates several limitations and requirements that allow the work of a visual artist to enjoy the protections of moral rights.

Sonny Bono Copyright Term Extension Act of 1998

The Copyright Term Extension Act of 1998 (CTEA), also known as the Sonny Bono Copyright Term Extension Act, lengthened the copyright term for individuals from fifty years (seventy-five years in the case of anonymous or pseudonymous works and works made for hire) to seventy years after an author's death (ninety-five years from date of first publication or 120 years from creation in the case of anonymous or pseudonymous works or works made for hire). In addition, the term for works published before January 1, 1978, and still in copyright protection on October 27, 1998, was extended to ninety-five years. Thus, CTEA affected copyrights existing as of the effective date and those created after the effective date.

Before the extension, certain works (including certain Mickey Mouse copyrights) were scheduled to enter the public domain in 1998. Now, no copyrighted works will enter into the public domain in the United States before January 1, 2019, when the copyright on works created in 1923 expires. But works created before 1923 are now in the public domain.

In 2003, the constitutionality of CTEA was challenged unsuccessfully in the Supreme Court in the case of *Eldred v. Ashcroft*. The named plaintiff, Eric Eldred, who is a publisher of works in the public domain and co-founder of the Creative Commons, argued chiefly that CTEA violated the Constitution's "limited Times" requirement (see page 6 for creators to control the disposition of their work and that the extension effectively guarantees an unlimited term of protection.

It is interesting to note that even the Register of Copyrights, Marybeth Peters, expressed the opinion that the current copyright term is probably too long and that Congress probably made a mistake, when she spoke at a November 5, 2005, symposium on intellectual property at the University of North Carolina Law School. When you consider the reality that the great majority of copyrights lose their economic value within two to ten years after publication, it is not hard to see that only the wealthiest and most profitable copyright owners (the Disneys of the world) actually benefit from such long copyright terms. Only time will tell whether terms for future works are reduced or whether a push for another copyright extension will come sometime around 2018 just before the works of 1923 are scheduled to enter the public domain.

Digital Millennium Copyright Act

Congress enacted another significant amendment to the Copyright Act, the Digital Millennium Copyright Act (DMCA), which President Clinton signed into law on October 28, 1998. The DMCA is made up of the World Intellectual Property Organization (WIPO) Copyright Treaty, the WIPO Performances and Phonograms Treaty, the Online Copyright Infringement Liability Limitation Act, the Computer Maintenance Competition Assurance Act, and the Vessel Hull Design Protection Act. Although substantive discussion of the intricacies of these various treaties and acts is well beyond the scope of this book, you should know that the DMCA sought to bring the body of copyright law in line with unique technological advances like software and the Internet. As it did with the Berne Convention, Congress made it clear that DMCA was not self-executing and that no further rights were granted other than those expressly provided in the law.

The DMCA addresses the unique concerns of copyright in the digital age, including the relative ease of large-scale infringement of perfect copies of digital and related electronic works, and it clarifies the scope of protection and penalties for infringement of such works. The DMCA generally makes it illegal to evade anti-piracy measures or to manufacture, sell, or distribute devices that assist others in circumventing such measures. The DMCA also provides exemptions to certain entities like libraries and educational institutions under certain circumstances, and limits the liability of Internet service providers and online service providers (like universities) for copyright infringement of users (provided they have an anti-infringement policy, take reasonable steps to implement the policy, notify users of the policy, and take down the offending material after receiving notice of the infringement).

Protecting Ideas

Copyright law expressly excludes ideas from its protection. *The American Heritage Dictionary* defines an idea as "something, such as a thought or conception, that potentially or actually exists in the mind as a product of mental activity." Therefore, the *idea* of writing a book about, for instance, a falsely accused prisoner who escapes from jail to prove his innocence and find the real killer cannot be protected under the Copyright Act. But the act does protect a written manuscript based on that idea. This conclusion makes sense in light of the way copyright is created. Copyright protection exists the moment an original and creative artistic or literary expression is *fixed* in a tangible form. Until an idea is fixed in a writing or recording, it is just that—an idea. Once fixed in a tangible form, the expression (assuming, of course, that it is also original and has some modicum of creativity) is protected by copyright.

It is not correct, however, to assume that an idea can never be protected. In fact, the protection of ideas is critical in situations where, for instance, you submit a book proposal to a publisher, pitch a screenplay to a producer or studio, or brainstorm with a collaborator about potential story lines. In such situations, ideas may be protectable under state law related to theories of contract (a nondisclosure agreement, for example), property, or in some cases, misappropriation.

2 The Specifics of Copyright Ownership

Copyright law protects your exclusive right to exploit (use productively) your original artistic or literary work. Copyright law was written to encourage the free exchange of ideas and to stimulate the progress of "useful arts," progress that benefits society. The theory behind the law is that the progress of useful arts is in the best interest of society but that creative individuals will not freely share their work without some say over how it is used. (To learn more about the history of copyright, see chapter 1.)

The federal Copyright Act provides copyright protection to "authors" (creators) of "original works." The act covers literary, dramatic, musical, artistic, dramatic, choreographic, pictorial, sculptural, and audiovisual works, and certain other creative works of an intellectual nature. Copyright protection is available for both published works (those made available to the public) and unpublished works (those shared with only a few or not at all).

When Copyright Ownership Begins and How Long It Lasts

Copyright exists *automatically* when a work is created. For the purposes of copyright law, a work is created when it is fixed in a copy or phonorecord for the first time. By "copy" the law means material objects—such as books, manuscripts, electronic files, Web sites, e-mail, sheet music, musical scores, film, videotape, or microfilm—from which a work can be read or visually perceived either directly or with the aid of a machine or device. Phonorecords are material objects such as cassette tapes, CDs, or LPs, but not motion picture soundtracks on which sounds are recorded and which combine moving images and sound. Thus, for example, a song (the work) can be fixed in sheet music (copies) or on a CD (phonorecord) or both. If a work is created over a period of time, the copyright applies automatically to whatever part is fixed on a particular date. So as soon as you write the first two paragraphs of your book, whether by hand on paper or by keying them into a computer, those paragraphs are immediately and automatically copyrighted—even if you don't get around to writing the third paragraph until a week or a year later.

The duration of copyright depends on when a work is created and always runs through the end of the calendar year in which it expires. And as you will see, the rules for older works can get pretty tricky. Review the Copyright Protection Timetable on page 41 to help you figure out when certain works may fall into the public domain. Here's a quick rundown of the general rules.

For works created on or after January 1, 1978, copyright lasts for the life of the author plus seventy years after the author's death. If there is more than one author, copyright lasts for seventy years after the death of the last survivor of all joint authors. For works created anonymously or under a pseudonym and for works made for hire, copyright lasts ninety-five years from the year of first publication or 120 years from the year of creation, whichever ends first.

For works created but not published or registered before January 1, 1978, copyright lasts, again, for the life of the author plus seventy years and in any case would not have expired before December 31, 2002. If the work was published before December 31, 2002, copyright will not expire before December 31, 2047. And for works published before January 1, 1978, still in their original or renewal term of copyright, copyright is extended to ninety-five years from the date that copyright was originally secured.

 Copyright protection is not available for any work of the United States government (for example, any publication created by a governmental agency, like the Copyright Office), but the United States government may receive and hold copyrights transferred to it by assignment, bequest, or otherwise. Therefore, just because a publication appears on a government Web site, it is not necessarily unprotected by copyright.

Showing the World That You Own Your Work

To demonstrate to the world that you own your work, you should use a copyright notice. The notice should contain all of the following three elements:

❑ *The symbol,* which for printed material is the letter "C" in a circle— ©; or, for CDs, audio tapes, and LPs, the letter "P" in a circle— ℗. Instead of the symbol you may use the word "Copyright" or the abbreviation "Copr."

❑ *The year* in which the work is first published. If your work is a compilation or a derivative that includes previously published material, use the year in which *you* first publish it. If your work consists of a picture, graphic, or sculpture, with or without accompanying text, and it is reproduced on greeting cards, postcards, stationery, jewelry, dolls, toys, or any useful article, no date is necessary. If your work is unpublished, use the year of creation and the phrase "Unpublished work" before the copyright symbol in the notice.

❑ *The name* of the copyright owner.

The copyright statement would then look like this:

© 2007 by Patsi Pen

Note that if your work is unpublished but copies leave your control, your notice should look like this:

Unpublished work. © 2007 by Patsi Pen

You should also consider including the phrase "All rights reserved". This phrase lets the public know that you have reserved each right in the bundle of rights that copyright contains. In that case, the copyright statement would look like this:

© 2007 by Patsi Pen

All rights reserved

Although use of the copyright notice is not required by law, it is still important that it appear in all copyrighted works because the notice informs the public that the work is protected by copyright, identifies the copyright owner, and shows the year of first publication. Notice is even more important in the online context (for more information about protecting your work online see chapter 4). Note, however, that a copyright notice is still required by law for works that were published before 1989 (see chapter 1). Furthermore, if your copyright is infringed and a proper notice of copyright appears on the published copy to which the infringer had access, then he or she cannot argue that the infringement was innocent. Innocent infringement can occur only when the infringer did not realize that the work was protected.

Without the copyright symbol on my manuscript, I won't have any copyright protection.

This is false. In 1989, the United States joined the Berne Convention for the Protection of Literary and Artistic Works, which is an international copyright treaty that requires all member countries to eliminate formal requirements as a condition to copyright protection. As a result, you *do not* have to use the copyright symbol or notice, or even register your copyright with the Copyright Office in order to create a protectable copyright interest. Copyright in original works of authorship exists as soon as the work is fixed in a tangible form.

What a Copyright Owner Has the Right to Do

In general, the Copyright Act gives a copyright owner the exclusive right to do and to authorize others to do (or preclude others from doing) the following:

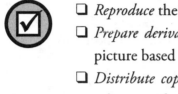

- ❑ *Reproduce* the work (make copies)
- ❑ *Prepare derivative works* based on the original (create a motion picture based on a novel or a novel based on a motion picture)
- ❑ *Distribute copies* of the work to the public (publish) by sale or other transfer of ownership, or by rental, lease, or lending
- ❑ *Perform the work publicly* (a public reading)
- ❑ *Display the work publicly* (hang a painting in an art gallery)
- ❑ *Perform the work publicly by means of a digital audio transmission (DAT)*, in the case of sound recordings

Collectively, these rights are often referred to as an author's exclusive bundle of rights. Let's look at each of these rights in closer detail.

Right to Copy

Because of the term "copyright," the right to copy is the most obvious right in the bundle of rights. The Copyright Act provides that copyright owners have the exclusive right to make copies of their work. With this right comes the right to allow others to make copies of their work.

Right to Make Derivative Works

One of the more valuable but lesser known rights in the bundle is the right to make derivative works. This means that you can create a screenplay based on your book or create a song from a poem or create a sculpture based on a photograph and so forth. Basically, this right allows you to update and revise your work (adding or deleting copyrighted elements) or re-create it in a different medium. Arguments against copyright infringement based on the derivative works right are that (1) the new creation is so different as to be transformative or (2) that the new work is a parody or (3) that some other fair-use exception applies. Nonetheless, you should take great care when basing your work on the work of others without their permission to do so.

Right to Distribute

A copyright owner has the exclusive right to make the first public distribution of the work—by sale, gift, loan, rental, lease, or other public transfer. But once that initial distribution of a copy is completed, the copyright owner cannot control how a particular copy is used thereafter. For this reason, it is OK for others to sell your book through Amazon Marketplace, for example, even though it competes directly with sales on the main product page. The same rule applies to sales on eBay. In fact, a person's right to dispose of his or her used property is the cornerstone of eBay's success. Thus, when the transfer of ownership in a copy of a book, piece of artwork, or other literary or artistic item is completed, the rights to control that copy also are transferred, regardless of how the copyright owner of the work itself may feel about such transfer.

Right to Perform and Display Publicly

The copyright owner's exclusive rights to perform and to display the work publicly do not apply only to for-profit situations but to all situations, including direct performance and display or by means of some device or process. In the literary context, this usually means reading a literary work aloud.

The Copyright Act defines a performance or display as public if it occurs "at a place open to the public or at any place where a substantial number of persons outside of a normal circle of a family and its social acquaintances is gathered." The legislative history of the 1976 version of the Copyright Act explains that a gathering of an individual's social acquaintances is generally regarded as private and not public. Additionally, routine meetings of businesses and governmental personnel are generally excluded, and case law seems to indicate that the word "publicly" indicates a gathering of a substantial number of people. Of course, there is no bright-line test or specific number, and thus whether a performance or display is public is decided case by case.

Scope of Copyright Protection

The Copyright Act protects only original works of authorship fixed in a tangible medium of expression now known or later developed, from which they can be perceived, reproduced, or otherwise communicated, either directly or with the aid of a machine or device. Works of authorship consist of the following categories:

- ❑ Literary works, and characters in some cases (as explained on page 16)
- ❑ Musical works, and any accompanying words
- ❑ Dramatic works, and any accompanying music
- ❑ Pantomimes and choreographic works

❑ Pictorial, graphic, and sculptural works
❑ Motion pictures and other audiovisual works
❑ Sound recordings
❑ Architectural works

A Note about Fictional Characters: You should be aware of two primary intellectual property laws regarding fictional characters, copyright and trademark:

1. Copyright protects original and creative artistic and literary works. As I said earlier, copyright allows the owner to (1) copy, (2) distribute copies, (3) make derivative works, for example, by turning a book into a screenplay, (4) perform the work publicly, and (5) display the work publicly. So copyright is actually a bundle of rights. But the owner cannot protect generic characters in a story that merely add color (for example, "Fannie, the sassy diner waitress who served us a stack of pancakes" or "Reginald, the distinguished businessman seated next to me on the plane"); however, lead characters like Stella in *How Stella Got Her Groove Back* or James Bond would be protected by copyright law. This also refers to artistic renderings in comic books, for instance. So you can't protect a stick figure or the name of a commonplace, peripheral character in a book or title of a book. On the other hand, courts have consistently extended copyright protection to graphic characters (those typically found in comic books, graphic novels, and cartoons) and fictional characters (meaning human beings who are created with words and without a pictorial rendering—at least initially—like James Bond or Austin Powers). In the case of graphic characters, courts have held that copyright extends to those characters that have sufficient original and creative characteristics to be distinctive characters (meaning not merely a drawing but a character with a name, features, and speech or other means of communication). Successful court battles to protect copyrighted characters have been fought over characters like Batman, Mickey Mouse, Superman, and Betty Boop. Such characters should not be confused with drawings of characters that have no features other than their graphic representations. In those cases, the drawings could certainly be copyrighted as visual art with Copyright Form-VA.

2. A second law that may apply and protect a fictional or graphic character is trademark law. Trademark law grants the owner the exclusive right to use a word, phrase, logo, design, sound, and so forth in connection with the sale of goods or services. But there is a fair-use exception for literary and artistic purposes in writing; otherwise these rules would stifle creativity. The exception applies as long as it is clear that the owner of a particular trademark is not the source of the book and has not endorsed it in any way.

This exception will be addressed—and, some writers' advocates say, affected negatively—by the Trademark Dilution Revision Act (HR 683), a bill that has passed both the House and the Senate. The stated purpose of the bill is to revise the Trademark Act of 1946 to clarify Congress's intentions regarding the section that deals with trademark dilution, that is, becoming too commonplace to warrant exclusivity. If signed into law, this amendment will further protect famous, distinctive trademarks from dilution.

In an e-mail to its members on February 14, 2006, the Authors Guild warned that this bill would weaken protections for free expression. The concerns seem to stem from the fact that while a major court case held that dilution law applies only to actual dilution, the new law would apply to situations in which a use is likely to cause dilution. The versions that have passed both the House and Senate claim to exclude from liability (1) fair use (nominative and descriptive), (2) product comparisons in the commercial context, and (3) noncommercial uses of famous marks. As of this writing, a joint committee of representatives and senators has convened to work out differences in their respective versions. When a final version is complete, the bill will be presented to the president to be signed into law.

The bottom line is that you can certainly mention fictional and graphic characters in your writing without violating copyright and trademark law, but you cannot use your own literary interpretation to develop different scenarios for those characters. So a new book about the life and times of James Bond or your own version of a Superman comic book will likely elicit a nasty cease-and-desist letter from the owner and maybe even a more onerous response.

The Elements of Copyrightable Works

As noted above, fundamental principles of copyright law require that works be original and fixed in order to qualify for copyright protection.

Originality: Copyrightable works must be original; that is, the work (story, song, poem, drawing, movie, and so forth) must be of the author's own independent creation. The originality requirement has a low threshold and *does not* require uniqueness, ingenuity, or any particular quality. The work must just be created independently and not copied from someone else's work. So in theory, two people could create the exact same work and both would receive copyright protection for their work as long as the work was original and not copied.

Part of the originality requirement is the condition that the work be creative. The creativity condition is minimal at best, requiring only that the work be more than a recitation of facts, numbers, graphs, and so forth. For example, a list of ingredients in a cookbook does not qualify for copyright protection. But a description of the process of combining ingredients is probably sufficient to qualify for copyright protection.

Fixation: An author's creation must be fixed in a tangible medium of expression and therefore capable of being perceived and, of course, copied. For instance, copyright does not exist until a story is written, typed, or recorded. The fixation may be viewed by way of a machine such as a computer, projector, digital camera, scanner, or even a machine that has not yet been created. But an idea is not protected by copyright; and a procedure, process, system, method of operation, concept, principle, or discovery is not protected by copyright either, regardless of the form in which it is expressed, illustrated, or perceived. Also, a live performance that is not fixed in a tangible form (written or recorded) is not protected by copyright law. So it's a good idea to write out or record a speech before you give it. But simultaneous fixation, such as a live broadcast of a sporting event, is protected by copyright.

What Copyright Does Not Protect

Despite the broad protection of copyright law, it does not protect the following things:

- ❏ Works that have *not* been fixed in a tangible form of expression (for example, choreographic works that have not been notated or recorded, or improvisational speeches or performances that have not been written or recorded)
- ❏ Titles of books and other works, proper names (including Web site domain names), short phrases, and slogans; familiar symbols or designs; mere variations of typographic ornamentation, lettering, or coloring; mere listings of ingredients or contents
- ❏ Ideas, procedures, methods, systems, processes, concepts, principles, discoveries, or devices, as distinguished from descriptions, explanations, or illustrations
- ❏ Works consisting entirely of information that is common property and containing no original authorship (for example, standard calendars, height and weight charts, tape measures and rulers, and lists or tables taken from public documents or other common sources)

Joint Ownership of Copyright: How Copyright Applies to Collaborators

Many creative people join forces to create a single literary or artistic work. For example, writers and illustrators may work together to create a children's book, a celebrity and a professional writer may team up to write the celebrity's autobiography, or a songwriter and composer may collaborate to create a song. When two or more writers or other creative people collaborate to create a copyrighted work and intend that their individual contributions be combined into a single interdependent work, by default, all of the contributors share equally in ownership of the copyright. This is true even if the participants contribute different parts to the whole or exert unequal effort (as when a celebrity lends her name to a project but the writer actually creates the manuscript).

Of course, the collaborators can (and should) enter into a written agreement that details specifically who owns what; how much money (if any) each contributor will receive; who is responsible for what; what happens if a collaborator dies, becomes disabled, or does not stay with the project to its completion; how the credits will appear; and in what name or names the copyright will be registered. In my law practice, I have seen the best of friends (and even relatives) turn into mortal enemies and ruin a project that had great potential and strong chances for publication and success because each person had a different understanding about who would do what, how much money each would receive, and how the business and artistic decisions would be handled. These problems resulted because the devilish details were not ironed out in writing before the collaborators started the project. These matters are covered in greater detail in my books *Literary Law Guide for Authors* and *Contracts Companion for Writers*. But for purposes of this discussion, just remember that unless the collaborators agree otherwise, they will all share joint ownership of the copyright.

3 Copyright Registration: Why, When, and How

Registration of your copyright creates a public record of the facts and circumstances pertaining to it. While registration is *not* necessary for copyright protection, it *is* necessary for other reasons.

Why You Should Register

You must register copyright in your work if you want to file an infringement suit in court. In addition, if you register, the Copyright Act gives you the following advantages:

❑ If registration is made before or within five years of publication, registration establishes prima facie evidence in court of the validity of the copyright and of the facts stated in the registration certificate.

❑ If registration is made within three months after publication of the work or before an infringement of the work, you may receive statutory damages and awards of attorney's fees in court actions. Otherwise, only an award of actual damages and profits is available to the copyright owner. As a practical matter, it is often very difficult to prove actual damages; thus statutory damages and attorney fees are a valuable benefit of registration.

❑ You can record the registration with the U.S. Customs Service for protection against the importation of infringing copies.

Contrary to popular belief, the Copyright Office ordinarily does not compare copyright registration forms with existing deposit copies or registration records to determine whether works submitted for registration are similar to any material for which a registration of copyright already exists. Therefore, the records of the Copyright Office may contain any number of registrations for works describing or illustrating the same underlying idea, method, or system.

When You Should Register

The question of when in the creative process a person should register the copyright is a good one, and one that does not necessarily have a precise answer. The "lawyerly answer" is based on the benefits of timely registration defined in the Copyright Act: you should register *before* your work is infringed and within three months of publication. This advice, of course, is not exactly helpful because you certainly cannot predict when your work might be infringed, and some work is never "published." Accordingly, I recommend the following guidelines:

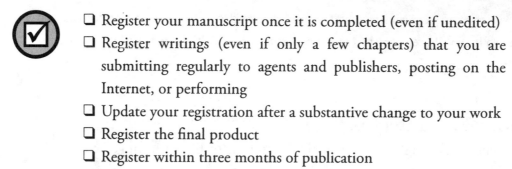

    ❑ Register your manuscript once it is completed (even if unedited)
    ❑ Register writings (even if only a few chapters) that you are submitting regularly to agents and publishers, posting on the Internet, or performing
    ❑ Update your registration after a substantive change to your work
    ❑ Register the final product
    ❑ Register within three months of publication

How to Register

So now that we have covered why and when writers should register copyrighted works, let's get to the actual process of registration. For the original registration of your book, manuscript, poetry, other text, or other artistic work, send an application form ☉, a nonrefundable filing fee ($45 as of July 1, 2006) for each application, and at least one nonreturnable sample of the work being registered to the Copyright Office. All three items should be submitted in the same package; an incomplete submission will not be processed and may be returned. You can contact the Copyright Office for specific deposit requirements, which means what kind and how many physical copies of your particular work the Copyright Office will require for review. Deposit requirements vary according to the type of work and whether it is published or unpublished. For contact information, see page 26 at the end of this chapter.

"Registration" with Writer's Organizations: Registering your work with a writer's guild or organization does *not* constitute registration under copyright law, unless the guild or organization (1) specifically states otherwise *and* (2) provides you with a registration certificate from the Copyright Office. In fact, you should register your copyright with the Copyright Office before submitting it to anyone or any organization. Organizations like the Writer's Guild of America allow writers to archive their scripts in the organization's database, which the organization refers to as "registration." Although archiving your work with a guild or organization may be beneficial in certain writing genres—as evidence within that circle that your work existed on a certain date and is available

to be developed—guild and organization registration should never replace registering your copyright with the Copyright Office at the Library of Congress.

A Word about Delivery of Mail to the Copyright Office: Because of the events of September 11, 2001, and its aftermath, the Copyright Office implemented new guidelines for receipt of deliveries. Mail sent to the Copyright Office is now screened off-site prior to arrival on Capitol Hill. This process can add three to five days to the delivery time for all mail sent to the Copyright Office. Additionally, the Copyright Office no longer accepts on-site deliveries from commercial couriers and messengers, but will accept such deliveries at an off-site location. The address for courier deliveries is listed in the Copyright Office contact information on page 26.

Tracking Your Copyright Application: To track your copyright application materials, be sure to send all correspondence via certified or registered mail and request a return receipt, or send via a private carrier. Also, never *ever* send the only copy of your work because it cannot be returned to you.

Types of Application Forms: The following application forms, which are the most relevant for writers, are all reproduced in Appendix B and on the CD-ROM.

Form TX	for published and unpublished nondramatic literary works
Form PA	for published and unpublished works of the performing arts (musical and dramatic works, pantomimes and choreographic works, motion pictures and other audiovisual works)
Form SE	for serials, works issued or intended to be issued in successive parts bearing numerical or chronological designations (Issue 1, 2, 3, etc. or Fall Issue, Spring Issue, etc.) and intended to be continued indefinitely (periodicals, newspapers, magazines, newsletters, annuals, journals, etc.)
Form SR	for published and unpublished sound recordings
Form VA	for published and unpublished works of the visual arts (pictorial, graphic, and sculptural works, including architectural works)

Effective Date: Copyright registration is effective on the date the Copyright Office receives all of the required elements in acceptable form.

Evidence of Application and Registration: If you apply for copyright registration, you will not receive an acknowledgment that your application has been received because the Copyright Office receives more than six hundred thousand applications each year. But a Copyright Office staff member will call or send a letter if further information is needed. You will receive a certificate of registration in about four or five months, indicating that the work has been registered; or, if the application cannot be accepted, you will receive a letter explaining why it has been rejected.

Correcting an Error in the Original Application: To correct an error in a copyright registration or to add information, you must file a supplementary registration form—Form CA—with the Copyright Office. The current filing fee for Form CA is $100.

Will an ISBN (International Standard Book Number) protect my copyright if it has not yet been registered?

No. As stated above, copyright exists from the moment a creative and original literary or artistic work is fixed in a tangible form. The only way to secure the additional protections offered by the Copyright Act is to register the copyright with the Copyright Office.

The Poor Man's Copyright or Mail Myth

I am sure you have heard of it. Virtually every writer has. And maybe you are among the considerable number of writers and industry professionals who not only believe the poor man's copyright myth but also repeat it as if it were the law. This is the most pervasive and destructive myth in the publishing industry. The poor man's copyright, also known as the mail myth, is the mistaken belief that a copyright is created or somehow protected when you send a copy of the work to yourself in the mail. If you learn nothing else from this book, you must learn this: the mail-yourself-the-manuscript-and-then-you'll-be-protected belief is a myth. It is simply not true, and I do not want anyone who reads these words to perpetuate this myth for one more moment. Rest assured, the only thing you will prove when you mail your work to yourself is that the post office is still in the business of delivering mail.

The mail myth evolved in the days before the 1989 amendment to the Copyright Act. Under prior copyright law (see chapter 1 for a brief history of copyright law), authors were required to include a copyright symbol on their work in order to create a copyright. Many rights were lost under the old law because of the strict requirement of the copyright symbol and other formalities. Writers believed that the only way to prove that the work existed on a particular date was to mail a copy to themselves. But these days this is neither necessary nor helpful when it comes to actually registering your work. This statement is confirmed by the Copyright Office and can be reviewed at the FAQ (frequently asked questions) page of the Copyright Office Web site, www.copyright.gov.

Simply put, the action of mailing a copy of your manuscript to yourself does not offer any additional protection beyond that which already exists once your idea is fixed and thus your work is created. Additionally, it does not constitute a registration of your copyright. A question I've been asked repeatedly over the years in response to my attempts to dispel the mail myth is this: "But doesn't the postmark prove that my work existed on a certain date? Couldn't this postmark be my 'smoking gun' to prove I am the owner of the work contained in the unopened envelope?" Even if a postmarked manuscript has some evidentiary value, the Copyright Act requires you to register your copyright *before* you have the right to file an infringement suit. There is no way to present your "smoking gun" without first securing your copyright registration.

But registration is easy (no need for a lawyer) and inexpensive (only $45 as of this writing)—a small price to pay to preserve valuable rights (think of it as the cheapest insurance policy you'll ever qualify for). So use the same stamps you would have used to mail your work to yourself and mail a copyright form, fee, and sample to the Copyright Office instead.

Preregistration of Certain Works

As a result of the Artists' Rights and Theft Prevention Act of 2005 (Title I of the Family Entertainment and Copyright Act), and in order to combat rampant piracy of unreleased projects in the entertainment industry, the Copyright Office adopted regulations allowing preregistration of certain unpublished works while they are being prepared for commercial distribution. The types of works that qualify for preregistration are those that have had a history of prerelease infringement, like highly anticipated movies, CDs, computer games and programs, and books. Preregistration does not apply to mere ideas that are not yet in the process of creation; for example, the idea for a book of which no part has been written down or saved as a word processing file cannot be preregistered. But the final work does not have to exist in physical format. For instance, a publishing company could register chapter outlines for the next Harry Potter book even though no chapters had yet been written and the actual book did not yet exist.

It is important to remember that preregistration is *not* registration, and preregistered works must be registered when the work is published. Also, preregistration is *not* necessary for the great majority of works. You should consider preregistration only if you think your work is likely to be infringed *before* its release (like the *Harry Potter* series book), and you have started the work but not yet completed it. So be sure to review the rules and requirements carefully at www.copyright.gov before seeking preregistration.

In general, to qualify for preregistration protection, (1) the work must be unpublished; (2) creation of the work must have begun; (3) the work must be a motion picture, sound recording, musical composition, book, computer program, or advertising photo; and (4) the work must be in the process of being prepared for commercial distribution. In the case of literary works, the Copyright Office requires the claimant to verify that he or she has a reasonable expectation that the work will be commercially distributed in the form of a book.

To preregister, you must submit an application online at eCO (the electronic Copyright Office) and pay a $100 fee.

Copyright Office Contact Information

- ❏ Mailing address:
    Library of Congress
    Copyright Office
    Reference & Bibliography Section LM-451
    101 Independence Avenue SE
    Washington DC 20559-6000
- ❏ Address for commercial courier and messenger deliveries:
    Congressional Courier Acceptance Site (CCAS)
    2nd and D Streets NE
    Washington DC
- ❏ Internet address: www.copyright.gov
- ❏ Public Information Office (live and recorded information): 202-707-3000 (8:30 a.m. to 5:00 p.m. Eastern time), Monday through Friday, except federal holidays
- ❏ Forms and Publications Hotline: 202-707-9100 (24 hours a day, 7 days a week). Request application forms and informational circulars by name or number. If you are unsure which form or circular to order, call the Public Information Office (listed above) instead.

❏ Fax-on-Demand: 202-707-2600 (24 hours a day, 7 days a week). Use only to request informational circulars. Application forms are not available by fax but can be downloaded at the Web site.

❏ TTY: 202-707-6737. For the hearing impaired. Messages may be left on the TTY line 24 hours a day. Calls are returned between 8:30 a.m. and 5:00 p.m. Eastern time, Monday through Friday, except federal holidays.

4 Copyright in the Digital Age

In chapters 2 and 3, I covered the basics of how copyright comes into existence, what a copyright owner has the right to do, and why and how to register your copyright. This chapter explores both the benefits and the challenges of digital technology as it relates to copyright formation and protection.

There is no doubt that new technology has had a substantial impact on the trade publishing industry. The changes brought about by technology are exciting and inspiring, but also troubling and challenging. A whole new world—the World Wide Web—offers unprecedented access to information, peers, and consumers. Continual accessibility to information and cut-and-paste technology have led to protection problems and widespread "sharing" and "use," which in turn have led to widespread infringement of perfect digital copies. This phenomenon has led to a generational shift in the appreciation of copyright and infringement, and a fundamental misperception that "if it's accessible on the Internet, it's *free*." And it's not just a sense that information on the Web is free: people who have that belief also believe they are somehow entitled to use the information. So as advances in technology challenge the effectiveness of existing copyright laws, the balance between an author's rights to control work and the public's right to benefit from creativity becomes more tenuous.

Protecting Your Work on the Internet

The question often arises as to how the Copyright Act applies to online works. As I've said, the Internet and other technological advances certainly do present numerous challenges to existing copyright law, and the law varies around the world. Thanks to the World Wide Web, information is accessible from every corner of the earth. But an online work is no different from its physical counterpart, except for the way the information is viewed or perceived. The same laws presented in chapters 1 and 2 apply to works displayed and distributed on the Internet, despite the all-too-prevalent erroneous assumption that if it's on the Internet it must be free for anyone and everyone to use.

Even though the same rights exist for physical and digital literary works, protecting your work on the Internet still presents a great challenge. This challenge persists because of the ease with which copyrighted works can be copied without distortion and distributed in the online context. So although copyright law as expanded by newer legislation like the Digital Millennium Copyright Act (see chapter 1) provides the legal framework necessary to help copyright owners enforce their copyrights online, the problem is that there is no system in place on the Internet to actively police and protect the rights of copyright owners in order to prevent unauthorized copying; there is nothing online comparable to a store clerk, who could stop someone who tried to copy pages of a book or magazine in the store, or an usher in a movie theater, who could stop someone who tried to record movies illegally during a showing.

Literary works consist of any creative work expressed with words, letters, or numbers, including computer programs. Some common examples for writers are letters, articles, books, and magazines. Online, we also have blogs, message boards and posts to discussion lists, e-mail messages, and e-newsletters.

When a Copy Infringes Online

One of the rights in a copyright owner's exclusive bundle of rights is the right to make copies of the work. This concept of copying, which is complex enough in regard to print, is even more complex when dealing with electronic copies and how they are created, viewed, and distributed online and with computers and handheld devices like Blackberries or Palms. For instance, you could purchase an e-book, download the file to your computer at home, and save it on the computer's hard drive or some other storage device. That would constitute one copy. Then you could burn the e-book onto a CD-ROM, and that would be another copy (one on the hard drive and one on the CD-ROM). Then you could copy that file onto your computer at work or to your laptop, and that would be yet another copy. Finally, you might think so much of this e-book that you attach it to an e-mail and send it to dozens of people who you think would benefit from the valuable information on it. If all of this copying is done without the copyright owner's permission, and no fair-use exception applies, then after the initial download and copying for personal use, you have infringed the work.

Registration of Online Works

There is no one form used specifically to register online works. In fact, the Copyright Office advises that the forms TX, PA, VA, and SR are mainly for office administrative purposes and therefore, technically, a work may be registered on any form.

Of course you should try to use the form most appropriate for your particular situation, and this decision depends on the nature of the online work you want to register. Here are some guidelines to help you choose the proper form:

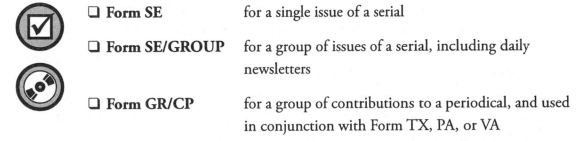

❑ **Form TX**   if text predominates, and there are few or no images or sounds appearing in the work

❑ **Form VA**   if pictures or graphics predominate the work, even if there are accompanying words

❑ **Form PA**   if audiovisual material (sound connected to images, like an online video) predominates

❑ **Form SR**   if sounds predominate (except the sounds that accompany and are intrinsic to an audiovisual work)

Some Web sites can be considered serials (recurring regularly, like a weekly e-newsletter or e-bulletin). In that case, choose from the following forms:

❑ **Form SE**   for a single issue of a serial

❑ **Form SE/GROUP**   for a group of issues of a serial, including daily newsletters

❑ **Form GR/CP**   for a group of contributions to a periodical, and used in conjunction with Form TX, PA, or VA

Your registration form should refer only to copyrightable information that is clearly identified in the form, has not been previously registered or published, and is not in the public domain. For published online works, the registration form should include only the content of the work actually published on the date given on the application.

Revisions and Updates

Problems of registration emerge when a Web site is updated frequently. The question arises as to whether it is necessary to register the site after each update. For individual works the answer, technically, is yes because there is no comprehensive registration to cover revisions published on different dates. Therefore, each daily update would have to be registered separately. As an attorney, I recommend that you do register each update to be fully protected. I recognize, however, that this would require much work and expense, and I acknowledge that most people don't follow this practice because they find it to be impractical. If you are like most people, then I suggest that you make it a practice to register your Web site every three months. If you do that, then you will be entitled to statutory damages and attorney fees if you ever have to sue someone for infringement. A different rule governs automated databases and serials because they qualify to use blanket registration (see below).

Automated Databases

Some frequently updated online works, like Amazon.com, are considered automated databases, because the Web sites consist of facts, data, and other pre-existing information organized in files for retrieval by means of a computer. When that is so, a group of updates to the database, whether published or unpublished, that cover up to three months within the same calendar year may be combined in a single, blanket registration. For more information about online databases, review Copyright Office Circular 65. (Note that all circulars are available at http://www.copyright.gov/circs/.)

E-Newsletters and Other E-Serials

Electronic versions of newsletters and serials are also protected by copyright and can be registered with the Copyright Office in a single registration covering multiple issues published on different dates. Group registration is available for works published weekly or less often (serials) and for newsletters published daily or more often than weekly, including those published online. The requirements vary, depending on the type of work. See Copyright Office Circular 62 for more information on serials. Note that group registration is available only for collective works, such as a collection of articles or an anthology, and not for electronic journals published one article at a time.

Blogs

The rules of copyright also apply to posts on blogs—both the blog owner's posts and comments by visitors. The owner holds the copyright to the post, and visitors own the copyright to their comments. There seems to be at least some implied license granted by a commenter to the blog owner to display the comment, but it is not clear how far that implied license reaches. But this implied license does not work the other way; nonetheless, reports from blog owners about rampant cut-and-paste infringement from their blogs for unauthorized posting to other blogs are far too common, and present a troubling development in the blogosphere.

To protect your blog and yourself from potential infringement claims from bloggers, always post your copyright information and instructions on how bloggers can use your posts, if at all. At a minimum, require that the post be copied in full and that it keep your copyright information intact. You may also want to ask for a link back to your Web site or blog. Of course, you should also consider registering blog posts; if your blog is a regular series (i.e., serial), then follow the registration guidelines for e-serials.

What Samples of Online Works to Send to the Copyright Office

For online works, the Copyright Office requires a deposit of one of the following:

> *Option A*: A computer disk, labeled with the name of the title and author, which contains the entire work, and a representative portion of the work in a format such as a printout, audiocassette, or video-tape that can be reviewed by the Copyright Office. If the work is five pages or less of text or artwork, or three minutes or less of music, sound, or audiovisual material, send the entire work as the deposit, and note that it is complete. If the work is longer than that, deposit five representative pages or three representative minutes.

> *Option B*: A reproduction of the entire work, regardless of length, in the format appropriate for the work being registered. For example, send a printout of a Web site made up of text or images, an audio-cassette of sound, or a videotape of audiovisual material. With this option, no computer disk is required.

These options apply when the work appears *online only*. If a work is published both online (for example, at the creator's Web site) and by the distribution of physical copies (an author's book, an artist's poster) in any format, then you must follow the regulations for depositing the physical copies.

For computer programs, databases, and works fixed in CD-ROM format transmitted online, the Copyright Office provides some guidance in Circulars 61 and 65. The office defines a computer program as "a set of statements or instructions to be used directly or indirectly in a computer in order to bring about a certain result." Deposit requirements for computer programs vary according to whether or not the work contains trade secrets. Trade secrets are defined by legal treatises as "any information that can be used in the operation of a business or other enterprise and that is sufficiently valuable and secret to afford an actual or potential economic advantage over others." If your work contains trade secrets, then you should include a cover letter stating that it does, along with the page containing the copyright notice, if any, and *one* of the following:

For entirely new computer programs

- ❑ The first and last twenty-five pages of source code with portions containing trade secrets blocked out
- ❑ The first and last ten pages of source code alone, with no blocked-out portions
- ❑ The first and last twenty-five pages of object code plus any ten or more consecutive pages of source code, with no blocked-out portions
- ❑ For programs fifty pages or less in length, the entire source code with trade-secret portions blocked out

For revised computer programs

- ❑ If revisions are present in the first and last twenty-five pages, any one of the four options above, as appropriate
- ❑ If revisions are not present in the first and last twenty-five pages, twenty pages of source code containing the revisions with no blocked-out portions, or any fifty pages of source code containing the revisions with some portions blocked out

For automated databases

- ❑ For a single-file database (which contains data records pertaining to a single common subject matter), the first and last twenty-five pages or, under a grant of special relief if you do not want to disclose trade secrets, the first and last twenty-five data records
- ❑ For multiple-file databases (which contain separate and distinct groups of data records), the first fifty data records from each file, or the entire file, whichever is smaller; or fifty pages of data records total under a grant of special relief. Also, you must include a descriptive statement that lists the title of the database; the name and address of copyright claimant; and the name and content of each separate file within the database, giving the subject matter, origin of data, and number of separate records within each file. For *published* multiple-file databases, also include a description and sample of the exact contents of any copyright notice used in or with the database (plus manner and frequency of display).

❑ For a revised database (either single or multiple file), fifty pages of records showing the revisions, or the entire revised portions if less than fifty pages

For works fixed in CD-ROM format, deposit one complete copy of the CD-ROM, along with any operating software or instruction manual, if applicable.

5 Using Other People's Work

Writers frequently want to quote from works written by others. Writers and publishers engage the services of editors, indexers, and others who may change or add words in the process of helping to create a finished work. What does the Copyright Act say in regard to such use of words written by others?

Fair Use

The doctrine of fair use significantly limits copyright protection. This doctrine permits use of copyrighted materials for certain purposes listed in the Copyright Act, such as criticism, comment, news reporting, teaching (including multiple copies for classroom use), scholarship, or research. While technically infringing on the copyright owner's rights, these uses are considered permissible; and such fair use can be used as a defense against a claim of copyright infringement. Fair use should not be confused with the concept of public domain, which is discussed on page 39.

Unfortunately, the proper application of fair use is at best difficult to determine. Contrary to popular belief, there is no specific number of words, lines, or notes of a copyrighted work that may safely be used without permission. Also, it is not sufficient simply to acknowledge the source of the copyrighted material. If your use is not fair use (and if no other exception applies), then you must obtain permission from the copyright owner. This is true not only for books and articles but for song lyrics, artwork, photographs, and other copyrighted works.

The music industry is especially protective and litigious when it comes to song lyrics and music copyrights. So borrower beware. The popular belief about quoting songs in incorrect. In most cases you must get a print license from the copyright owner if you quote song lyrics in your book or article, even if you want to use the quote in a textbook. Getting permission is relatively simple; it can be obtained with a short permissions request; see page 42 for details.

A certain number of words of copyrighted material can be used without the permission of the owner.

This myth among writers that using, say, 500 words or less of any copyrighted material is *always* fair use is just that: a myth. It is *not true*. In fact, copyright law does *not* set a precise amount of a copyrighted work that can be used without the owner's permission. The Copyright Act provides a series of factors to be considered to determine whether fair use exists.

How to Establish Fair Use

The Copyright Act provides four factors to be used in order to determine, on a case-by-case basis, whether fair use or infringement exists.

❑ *Character or Purpose of Use*: Allowable use consists of criticism (reviews), comment (reviews), news reporting, nonprofit teaching (classroom), scholarship (reference materials), noncommercial research (law review articles), and parody (as in the book *The Wind Done Gone*, by Alice Randall). Note that use for commercial purposes will not automatically preclude a finding of fair use. For example, compiling a book of movie reviews does not, in itself, defeat a fair-use argument. The key issue is whether use of the copyrighted work is transformative, meaning whether the use actually builds on the original work to create something new or whether the use is merely a verbatim recitation.

❑ *Nature of Copyrighted Work*: A court takes into consideration the type of work involved—for example, whether it is fiction or nonfiction, published or unpublished. Generally a court is less likely to find fair use when a work of fiction or fantasy is copied than when one dealing with facts and figures is copied, or when the work is unpublished or consists of private letters.

❑ *Amount and Substantiality of the Copied Work:* Although no set number of words determines fair use, a court will consider how much of the copyrighted work was used (in other words, did you use one word or a few words, or did you use a large portion of the whole work). Infringement can be found, however, even when only a few words are used if those words are the heart of the copyrighted work. On the other hand, copying an entire copyrighted work was held to be fair use in a few cases.

❑ *Effect on the Potential Market:* A court will ask whether use of the copyrighted work lessens the value of that work. If the use harms the copyright owner's ability to benefit financially from the copyrighted work, it is less likely that fair use exists. If, however, the quoted material is properly credited to the owner and that credit increases the likelihood of sales for the owner, then it is more likely that fair use exists.

Unfortunately, applying these four factors often raises more questions than it answers, and even a comprehensive analysis of the factors provides no absolute conclusions. Only a judge can make the ultimate decision as to whether a particular use is fair.

The Impact of New Technologies on Fair-Use Analysis: The fair-use doctrine was created at a time when print was the main mode of transmitting creative works. With new technologies that allow one person to store large amounts of information in digital form and transmit that same information in perfect condition to millions of people with a few clicks of the mouse, it is easy (and scary) to imagine the innumerable infringements of copyrighted work that exist every second of every day and that remain unpoliced and incapable of control. In light of this twenty-first-century reality, some scholars believe that the law lags far behind in closing the gap between yesterday's statutes and today's technology.

Public Domain

The concept of fair use should not be confused with the concept of public domain. In the former, copyright protection exists and a copyright infringement occurs, but fair use is a legal defense to infringement that "excuses" the violation. On the other hand, when a work is in the public domain it has no copyright protection, and anyone can freely use the work. Therefore, the public—rather than a particular individual or entity—owns the work.

A work might be in the public domain for one of four reasons: (1) the term of copyright protection has expired; (2) the author failed to fulfill a requirement (known as a formality) and therefore lost the right to receive copyright protection; (3) the work was created by the U.S. government or for some other reason is not protected by copyright law; or (4) the copyright owner actually dedicated the work to the public domain. As a rule of thumb, registered works created before 1923 are now in the public domain.

When a Work Enters the Public Domain

Different versions of the Copyright Act (see chapter 1) apply to different works, depending on when those works were created (if unpublished) or published. The Copyright Protection Timetable on page 41 is a useful guide for determining whether a work is in the public domain, assuming that you know the work's publication date.

Note: All copyright terms run through the end of the year in which they are to expire, so copyright of a work created on August 21, 2006, by an individual who dies in 2026, would last through December 31, 2096. All works created by U.S. government officers and employees in the scope of their employment are in the public domain from the date of creation.

Copyright Protection Timetable

Type of Work	Date Work Falls into the Public Domain
Unpublished in the U.S.	
Named authors who died before 1936	Now in the public domain, since copyright for these works lasts for the life of the author plus 70 years.
Anonymous and pseudonymous works, and works made for hire created before 1886	Now in the public domain, since copyright for these works lasts for 120 years from date of creation.
Unpublished works created before 1978 that were published after December 31, 2002	Now in the public domain if the author died before 1935.
If date of author's death is unknown	Now in the public domain if created before 1886, since copyright for these works lasts for 120 years from date of creation.
Published in the U.S.	
Works published before 1923	Now in the public domain.
Works published from 1923 through 1977 without a copyright notice	Now in the public domain.
Unregistered works published from 1978 to March 1, 1989, without a copyright notice	Now in the public domain.
Works published from 1923 through 1963 but not renewed	Now in the public domain.
Published outside the U.S.	
Works published before July 1, 1909	Now in the public domain.

Getting Permission to Use the Work of Others

To acquire permission from a copyright owner to use his or her copyrighted work in, for instance, your manuscript, you must use a permissions request. Perhaps you want to include a quotation or excerpt from another author's copyrighted work, or a photograph or an illustration, and your use would not be considered fair use (and we have already discussed how difficult it is to determine whether fair use exists). In that case, or even if fair use clearly exists, you should consider at least trying to get permission in writing so that if you face an infringement case down the line, you can establish a good-faith effort to secure permissions. It is not enough to believe you are right where copyright is concerned, especially in this litigious society. From a financial perspective, you still lose if you have to prove that you are right in court. Many authors and independent publishers do not have the financial means to battle with the music industry, for instance, which jealously guards its intellectual property—right or wrong (remember Napster).

Hunting down permission to use a quote a couple of months before you go to print is always a bad idea. You will likely find that the owner of the work you intend to use does not care as much about your deadlines as you do. And there is nothing worse than the pressure of printing and release deadlines looming over your head while you wait, at the last minute, to dot your i's and cross your t's. So the ultimate decision about if and when to seek permission often boils down to a matter of business as well as legality. You must assess the costs and benefits of choosing to seek permission and proceed accordingly. Also, when you sign a publishing agreement, you will often be required to obtain any necessary written permissions to use copyrighted material because the publisher does not want to be exposed to legal liability for infringement.

A permissions request should

- ❑ describe the copyrighted material with great specificity
- ❑ note the source of the material
- ❑ state whether the material has been previously published and, if so, state the date, author, publisher, and current owner
- ❑ include a grant of permission that specifically states how the material can be used, naming any limitations on use (if applicable)
- ❑ state whether the grant is exclusive or nonexclusive (and if nonexclusive, whether it is revocable or irrevocable)
- ❑ include specifications for copyright notice and credit
- ❑ include a declaration of control in which the owner expressly states that he or she is the sole owner and has the power to give

the requested permission, or if not the sole owner, how you should contact the other owners to get the necessary signatures. As a matter of efficiency, you should try to get all owners to sign off on the same permissions form.

Finding out how to reach the person who has the authority to grant permission to use pictures, quotes, and other copyrighted work can be difficult. Here are some possibilities:

- ❑ Copyright and permissions-request information is listed on the back of the title page in most books.

- ❑ The Copyright Clearance Center, Inc. (CCC)—www.copyright .com(not to be confused with the unrelated Copyright Office at www.copyright.gov)—is a licensor of text reproduction rights. Contact CCC to get permission to reproduce copyrighted content such as articles and book chapters in your journals, photocopies, course packs, library reserves, Web sites, and e-mail.

- ❑ National Writers Union (NWU) represents freelance writers in American markets. For permissions to use articles by freelance writers, contact NWU via the Publication Rights Clearinghouse: prc@nwu.org.

- ❑ Harry Fox Agency (HFA—National Music Publisher's Association) is the leading mechanical licensing, collections, and distribution agency for U.S. music publishers. Contact HFA at http://www .harryfox.com or 711 Third Avenue, New York, NY 10017 Tel: 212-370-5330, Fax: 646-487-6779.

- ❑ ASCAP (American Society of Composers, Authors and Publishers) is a performing-rights organization that licenses the rights of its member songwriters, composers, and publishers at www.ascap .com. It is a licensor of public performance rights and can be reached as follows:

> Internet licensing: weblicense@ascap.com
>
> Cable or satellite licensing: cablelicensing@ascap.com
>
> Television licensing: TVLicensing@ascap.com
>
> Radio licensing: radiolicensing@ascap.com
>
> General licensing: licensing@ascap.com

- ❑ BMI (Broadcast Music, Inc.) is a performing-rights organization that licenses the public performance rights of its member songwriters, composers, and publishers at www.bmi.com or 320 West 57th Street, New York, NY 10019-3790, 212-586-2000.

❑ SESAC (Society of European Stage Authors and Composers) is a performing-rights organization that licenses the public performance rights of its member songwriters, composers, and publishers at www.sesac.com.

❑ Icopyright.com is an online licensor of digital content (work published on the Internet) at www.icopyright.com.

❑ The Photographer's Index connects the public with owners of photographic works at www.photographersindex.com.

Work Made for Hire

As you know by now, a copyright generally exists in a work as soon as it is created in a fixed and tangible form. The creator of the work owns and controls the bundle of rights associated with copyright. An exception to that rule is the work-made-for-hire doctrine, in which the creator is not the owner for purposes of copyright protection. The Copyright Act provides strict guidelines that determine whether a work-made-for-hire situation exists.

Work made for hire can occur in two contexts: that involving employers and employees and that involving independent contractors. In the first, work made for hire is done by employees within the scope of their employment. In the second, an independent contractor is specially commissioned to perform work for one of the following purposes only:

❑ a contribution to a collective work
❑ a part of a motion picture or other audiovisual work
❑ a translation
❑ a supplementary work, which includes such things as forewords, editorial changes, and indexes
❑ a compilation
❑ an instructional text
❑ a test
❑ answer material for a test
❑ a sound recording
❑ an atlas

Furthermore, the work performed by the independent contractor is considered to be work made for hire only if the contractor and the hiring person both sign a contract *before* the work begins, stating that the work is made for hire.

Because the existence of work made for hire depends on the relationship of the parties involved, the first question to answer is whether the creator is an employee or an independent contractor.

Employee: In the employer-employee relationship, the employer controls the work product, work site, work schedule, and assignments; provides the equipment used to perform the work; pays the employee a regular salary and takes appropriate deductions; and so forth. For example, a staff writer is an employee of a newspaper company. In that situation, the newspaper company and not the staff writer owns the copyright of all work produced by the writer during his or her employment.

Independent contractor: Unlike employees, independent contractors maintain control over how the work they do is done. Independent contractors are in business for themselves. They provide their own equipment, and set their own hours and work schedule. They may refer to themselves as business owners, freelancers, self-employed, or consultants. They are their own bosses.

If you want an independent contractor to contribute to your product, and you want to retain copyright to his or her contribution, then as stated earlier you must both sign a work-made-for-hire agreement before the work begins. To further protect your interests, make sure the agreement has an assignment provision to assign the creator's rights to you in case the work-made-for-hire provisions fail to secure copyright to you for any reason.

What Does Your State Say about Work Made for Hire? The discussion of work-made-for-hire agreements above is the law as stated in the federal Copyright Act and as such is a general statement about the law. But your state may provide additional requirements for such agreements. For example, under California law, creators who enter into a work-made-for-hire agreement are considered to be employees—not independent contractors—for purposes of workers' compensation and unemployment insurance. This has serious implications because the proposed owner would be required in California to carry workers' compensation insurance that covers the creator.

6 Writing about Real People and Real Life

Nonfiction writers write about real life and real experiences. Whether they are writing memoir, biography, or news reports, nonfiction writers tell a story—a real story. So there are certain legal issues that nonfiction writers in particular should be aware of—in addition to the other issues raised in this book—before, during, and after the writing process.

Nonfiction Writing

What differentiates fiction from nonfiction is that fiction is not real; it is made up; it comes from the writer's imagination. Nonfiction, on the other hand, is factual or at least represents the author's opinions based on facts. Nonfiction consists of many genres, such as history, philosophy, biography, and memoir.

Speaking of memoir, perhaps you've heard about the controversy surrounding the book *A Million Little Pieces* by James Frey, which was published in 2003 by Doubleday Books, a Random House imprint. The book was so compelling and provocative that it caught the attention of the media mogul Oprah Winfrey, who selected it as an Oprah Book Club Selection. In her show on October 26, 2005, titled "The Man Who Kept Oprah Awake at Night," Oprah celebrated Frey's graphic book, which Frey and Doubleday presented as a memoir. Oprah described it as a book "like nothing you've ever read before." Later, it was reported that Frey's supposed memoir, a work of nonfiction, contained lies and fiction. After feeling duped by Frey and the Doubleday editor Nan Talese, Oprah—during a live show on January 26, 2006—expressed regret and apologized for comments she made on *Larry King Live* in support of what she and Frey referred to as the "essential truth" of the book.

During that January 26 show, in response to Oprah's question about whether an editor should take any responsibility for the book's inauthentic nature, the editor Nan Talese replied, "Well, I can only tell you how the book came to me and how I read it. And I read the manuscript as a memoir. I thought it was this extraordinary story of a man with drug addiction going through the hell of both the addiction and the recovery and the process." She went on to say, "As an editor, do you ask someone, 'Are you really as bad as you are?'" Talese's implied question seems to be whether an editor should check the veracity of every detail of an author's memoir. Oprah's brilliantly simple answer was a resounding yes.

After Frey's lies were exposed on thesmokinggun.com, Doubleday posted an "Author's Note" on its Web site and included this note in all subsequent printings of this still-popular title. The note begins: "*A Million Little Pieces* is about my memories of my time in a drug and alcohol treatment center. As has been accurately revealed by two journalists at an Internet Web site, and subsequently acknowledged by me, during the process of writing the book, I embellished many details about my past experiences, and altered others in order to serve what I felt was the greater purpose of the book." Frey goes on to give his own definition of his purported memoir as "a combination of facts about my life and certain embellishments. It is a subjective truth, altered by the mind of a recovering drug addict and alcoholic."

A *New York Times* article quoted Frey as saying that he originally envisioned *A Million Little Pieces* not as a memoir but as a novel: "We were in discussions after we sold it as to whether to publish it as fiction or as nonfiction." And reports suggest that there had been some speculation as to whether Frey was pressured or even encouraged by the publisher to pursue the project as memoir.

Nonetheless, Doubleday also issued a separate statement expressing disappointment and regret that it backed Frey initially. That note says in part, "We bear a responsibility for what we publish, and apologize to the reading public for any unintentional confusion surrounding the publication of *A Million Little Pieces*."

So it seems that Frey, Doubleday, and Oprah have all covered their respective bases and did the necessary damage control to stem the tide of impropriety surrounding this topic. Only time will tell whether this is but another forgettable blip on the screen of life or whether the publishing industry will take heed and employ fact checking and legal vetting more often and with greater depth.

Incidentally, this controversy led me to investigate the difference between memoir and autobiography in order to help writers grasp the actual (or perceived) distinction. In response to a visitor's query about the memoir-autobiography distinction, WritersDigest.com answered: "autobiography focuses on the writer's entire life, whereas memoir focuses on a certain aspect of it."

So while an autobiography generally portrays an overarching timeline and myriad events throughout the author's life, a memoir usually is restricted to a particular theme or timeframe in the author's life and specific recollections related to that theme or time. And though a memoir may be closer to a journal than to journalism, it seems it must be truthful. Otherwise, it's fiction, a novel based (sometimes loosely) on a true story.

Now, let's take a look at three of the more important legal considerations that nonfiction writers should be familiar with: libel, and the rights of privacy and publicity.

Libel

Libel is the written form of defamation. Defamation has been defined as any written or oral untrue statement that injures a third party's reputation. The oral form of defamation is known as slander. The key to avoiding a claim of libel is to ensure that the facts are accurate and portrayed in the proper light. This does not mean that the information has to be complimentary or favorable, but it must be accurate and truthful. A person may be guilty of libel if he or she writes an untrue statement and conveys that written statement to the public negligently—meaning the person should have known that it was a false statement or should have verified its accuracy. If the subject of the writing is a famous person, then an actual bad motive must be proven as well. The truth is generally a complete defense to a claim of libel.

Privacy

Given the very nature of life, when writers seek to tell their life stories, the stories of other people must be told as well because those stories are often inextricably linked. Nowhere is this more evident than in the autobiography, biography, and memoir. There are two types of biography: authorized and unauthorized. As the name suggests, the authorized biography is done with the permission of the subject. The other is not.

The American Heritage Dictionary defines the right of privacy as "the quality or condition of being secluded from the presence or view of others." More simply put, it is the right to be left alone. The three generally recognized invasions of privacy are intrusion, unreasonable publicity, and false light.

Intrusion occurs when someone intentionally enters without permission into a place where one has a reasonable expectation of privacy. Intrusion involves issues such as hidden cameras or other surveillance methods, wire tapping, and searching someone's garbage. Therefore, when conducting interviews, you should always inform the subject that you are taping or otherwise memorializing the conversation. To further protect yourself, you should require all interviewees to sign a permission form authorizing you to tape the conversation and to use the content in all future editions of your literary work. In intrusion claims, a plaintiff is not required to show that the alleged intruder divulged the information obtained to the public. It is sufficient to show that the person entered a place where the plaintiff had a reasonable expectation of privacy (his or her home, for instance).

Unreasonable publicity (also known as public disclosure of private facts) occurs when intimate or embarrassing facts about a person are divulged to the public ("published," or made known publicly) in an unfair or irrational way. A court may find such publication to be unreasonable when the information is not of public interest or concern. And it is not enough to argue that the information is true. In fact, privacy laws are intended to protect against the publication of truthful but private information.

False light occurs when a person is portrayed in public in an extremely offensive way. The classic example is when an offensive caption appears beneath someone's picture, a caption that could leave a false and negative impression of the individual in the mind of a reasonable person. A false-light claim can also arise when essential facts are omitted: for example, when a reporter writes that a man was arrested for molesting his seven-year-old son but fails to report that all charges were subsequently dropped when it was discovered that the father was out of town during the incident; or when certain elements of a book are fictionalized but it is not clear what is fact and what is fiction, a situation that can be avoided with a clear, well-written disclaimer.

So, you might ask, when is it OK to discuss intimate facts? Writers are usually permitted to discuss facts that are generally known to the public (even a small circle of people) or facts that are considered newsworthy. But here's a general list of materials that are considered off limits without permission: private letters and e-mail (both of which are covered by copyright, with ownership held by the writer), information about sexual proclivities or sexual history, financial or medical information, and information about other private matters. When discussing the lives of noncelebrities, remember that it is even more difficult to establish that the information is of public concern or interest. The sex life of Bill Clinton or Kobe Bryant may be worthy of a tell-all unauthorized biography, but that may not be true of your ex-spouse, unless he or she also happens to be a public figure whose affairs would be considered of public concern or interest.

Publicity

The right of publicity is a person's exclusive right to use, and to prevent the unauthorized use of, his or her name, likeness, or other aspect of his or her persona (collectively referred to as persona) for commercial gain. The definition of "persona" goes beyond a person's image and can include words or sounds that are intended to remind the audience of the person, a look-alike, a nickname or phrase commonly associated with the person (like "the Donald" and "You're Fired!" for Donald Trump), and even a person's former name. Therefore, the potential for a right-of-publicity claim exists any time you use someone's persona (or even an imitation of it) in your book, article, or other literary or artistic work.

There is no federally protected right of publicity. This right is protected in some states by case law; in other states it is protected by statutes developed by legislative bodies. And some states do not protect this right at all. So you should definitely consult an attorney familiar with your local laws if you have specific questions about the right of publicity. But under a federal law known as the Lanham Act, a person may be able to establish a claim for the unauthorized use of his or her identity if it creates a false endorsement.

The two main exceptions to the right of publicity, the newsworthiness exception and the incidental-use exception, are based on the First Amendment's balance between free speech and the right of publicity.

The newsworthiness exception allows a person's name or likeness to be used in a news story without that person's consent as long as the use is considered to be of legitimate public interest or concern. Furthermore, the use cannot mislead the reader into thinking that the person endorses the article, newspaper, book, or whatever vehicle his or her persona appears in. A common way that writers can protect themselves when writing about others is to include a disclaimer making it clear that those others do not endorse the writing.

The exception for incidental use occurs when a person's name is merely mentioned or his or her likeness is used or referred to. If this exception did not exist, the right of publicity could very well stifle creativity. For instance, authors would not be able to authenticate a story line by referring to real people and places, whether in nonfiction or fiction.

Use of someone's persona may also be permissible if editorial in nature, that is, if used for news reporting or scholarship, or for cultural, historical, educational, political, or public interest reasons. The same consideration is given to artistic use in which an individual's name or likeness appears in a work of fiction that incorporates real people. Again, this use is probably permissible as long as the goal is artistic and of public interest and concern rather than for purely economic gain.

So here are some recommendations to consider. To avoid legal pitfalls of nonfiction writing, take care of the facts and make sure that they are accurate and documented and, if possible, verified by at least two independent sources. Also, make sure that you do not obtain factual information by invading someone's privacy and that you do not divulge information obtained by reason of a confidential relationship or a relationship protected by law, such as that of attorney-client or doctor-patient, or situations in which a confidentiality agreement is in place. Also, avoid using private letters and e-mail without permission. Change names and physical descriptions when possible to protect others while telling the story.

A Note about Historical Fiction

Historical fiction is a popular writing genre that generally incorporates fictional and historical characters in a specific, well-researched historical period and setting. The heart of good historical fiction rests in the soundness of the research and authenticity of the historical references. But historical fiction should include a well-written disclaimer stating that the work is one of fiction so readers will know that the plot was developed or history altered with the purposeful literary freedom of historical fiction—poetic license—and is not the result of inadvertent inattention or worse.

7 International Copyright

One of the most often asked questions about copyright is whether an artistic or literary work created in the United States is protected in other countries. The answer is a lawyerly one: it depends. A related question is whether there is an international law that protects copyrights in every country, and the short answer is no. How (and whether) a copyrighted work created in the United States is protected in another country depends on the laws of that country because there is no single body of law that protects all copyrights in all countries.

In general, most countries afford some protection to foreign works in their countries by way of certain international treaties and conventions joined by those other countries. The key is to determine whether the country at issue has volunteered to participate in mutually beneficial copyright relations with the United States. Check Copyright Office Circular 38a at http://www.copyright.gov/circs/ for a detailed listing of country participation in the various treaties and conventions. If the country does provide some protection via treaty or convention, then follow the applicable rules to protect your work in that country. If a country does not participate in any treaties or conventions, you may still be protected under that nation's copyright. If there is no copyright protection in that country for foreign works, then you are out of luck.

Ideally, you should confirm whether protection exists in other countries of concern to you before you publish because your rights may well depend on whether or not the work has already been published. If you have a question about protection of your work in other countries, you should contact an intellectual property lawyer familiar with international laws related to copyright.

The two main international copyright conventions are the International Union for the Protection of Literary and Artistic Property (Berne Convention) (see page 54) and the Universal Copyright Convention (UCC). These treaties set a minimum threshold of copyright protection for each nation that subscribes to them. And member countries have the discretion to provide even greater protections as long as they provide the fundamental protections. Countries may belong to more than one convention or other international agreement, so international copyright protection, like that in the United States, is a complex issue to unravel. Nonetheless, given our digital age and the now firmly established World Wide Web, you must have at least a basic understanding of international copyright issues in order to successfully protect and exploit copyright of your work abroad.

Berne Convention

The Berne Convention is known to commentators and intellectual-property experts as the foundation of modern international copyright law. Adopted in 1866, it is also the oldest major treaty involving international copyright protection. As I said earlier, at this time the Berne Convention has 161 members, including the United States and the great majority of the countries with which it trades.

The Berne Convention protects literary and artistic works regardless of their means of expression. It also establishes protection for moral rights (the rights of attribution and integrity), fixes a minimum duration of copyright protection (life of the author plus fifty years), and prohibits formalities such as use of the copyright symbol or copyright registration from being required *before* protection exists.

The minimum standards for protection under the Berne Convention consist of the exclusive right of the creator to translate, reproduce, publicly perform, adapt, alter, arrange, and publicly broadcast his or her creation. Again, the language of the Berne Convention makes it clear that these are threshold protections and that member nations may provide greater protection.

The Universal Copyright Convention

The Universal Copyright Convention (UCC), signed originally in Geneva in 1952 and revised in Paris in 1971 at the same time the Berne Convention was revised, is administered through UNESCO (the United Nations Educational, Scientific and Cultural Organization). Like the Berne Convention, the UCC sets minimum standards of protection that each member nation must include in its national law and must grant to citizens of other member nations. But it prescribes fewer protections than does the Berne Convention.

The UCC was created so that nations who were not signatories to the Berne Convention (because of its more comprehensive baseline requirements) could still participate in an international treaty that would afford some copyright protection. The participating nations include the United States, but that participation became much less important after the United States joined the Berne Convention in 1989.

Enforcement

While the Berne Convention and UCC are important in terms of setting the bar for international copyright protection, a major issue not adequately addressed by either treaty is that of enforcement. All the rights in the world mean nothing without an adequate means of enforcing them. In recognition of the limitations of enforcement mechanisms in international treaties, a new international trade agreement administered by the General Agreement on Tariffs and Trade (GATT)—and now by the World Trade Organization (WTO)—emerged in April 1994. Known as Trade Related Aspects of Intellectual Property Rights (TRIPS), it sets the minimum substantive standards of protection and enforcement for participating nations. TRIPS also provides exceptions for the first time in an international treaty. It expressly excludes ideas, procedures, methods of operation, and mathematical concepts from copyright protection. TRIPS requires "effective" enforcement of rights and certain baseline enforcement procedures and remedies, including certain administrative procedures, civil and criminal procedures and remedies, and border control. The enforcement requirements are tempered a bit because of the wide variance in the means of member nations (at varying levels of development) to create and maintain identical methods of enforcement. The bottom line is that member nations are required to take "effective action against any act of infringement . . . and remedies which constitute a deterrent to further infringements." Still, the system is far from perfect. In fact, on May 25, 2005, in a statement before the Subcommittee on Intellectual Property, of the Committee on the Judiciary, Marybeth Peters, the Register of Copyrights, concluded that "there remains, however, substantial work to be done in making sure that those structures provide *effective* enforcement of copyright."

8 How to Investigate the Copyright Status of a Work

There are several ways to investigate whether a work is protected by copyright or whether it is in the public domain. The easiest way to begin is to examine the work itself for the copyright notice information, place and date of publication, and author information, which can be found in most books on the back of the full-title page. The second way is to conduct a search of the Copyright Office catalog and other records either online at www.copyright.gov/records/ or in person. The third way is to have the Copyright Office conduct a search for you. In many cases you will need to use more than one way to conduct a comprehensive search, and even a comprehensive search may not be conclusive. Therefore, it may be important to contact an attorney before coming to any conclusions about your particular copyright status question.

The Copyright Office published the *Catalog of Copyright Entries* (*CCE*) in book form from 1891 to 1978 and in microfiche form from 1979 to 1982. Many libraries maintain copies of the *CCE,* and the *CCE* may be a good starting point for research. Because the *CCE* does not contain copyright assignment and other recorded documents, however, it cannot be the only method used to track copyright ownership conclusively. Also, while the *CCE* contains facts about copyright registration, it does not provide a verbatim account nor does it include contact information for the copyright claimant. Copyright registrations after 1978 are found online only, in the Internet databases of the Copyright Office at http://www.copyright.gov/records/.

Where to Search for Information about Registered Copyrights

The Copyright Office is in the Library of Congress James Madison Memorial Building, 101 Independence Avenue SE, Washington DC 20559-6000. Most Copyright Office records are open to public inspection and searching from 8:30 a.m. to 5:00 p.m., Eastern time, Monday through Friday, except federal holidays. The general public can conduct free searches of the card catalog, the automated catalog containing records from 1978 forward, record books, and microfilm records of assignments and related documents. Certain records, including correspondence files and deposit copies, can be accessed only by the Copyright Office itself, for a fee. You will find the Copyright Office fee schedule in Appendix B and on the CD-ROM accompanying this book. Be advised, however, that fees are subject to change; you can verify the actual amount of search fees at www.copyright.gov/.

The Copyright Office staff will search its records for you for a fee of $75 per hour. Based on the initial information you furnish, the office will provide an estimate of the total search fee, which you submit along with your request. The office will then proceed with the search and send you a typewritten report or, if you prefer, an oral report by telephone. In the case of search requests based on evidentiary requirements for a lawsuit, search reports can be certified on request for an extra fee of $80 per hour. Note that the search fee does not include the cost of additional certificates, photocopies of deposits, or copies of other Copyright Office records.

When It's Difficult or Impossible to Locate a Copyright Owner

Sometimes, despite your best intentions and efforts, it may be difficult or even impossible to identify or locate the copyright owner of an older work that you'd like to use in your own work. More than a few copyright owners do not register with the Copyright Office, and those who do register may not record the copyright transfer (known as an assignment) or update those records of transfers if and when things change. (Check with your publisher to make sure that your registrations are complete and correct!)

Copyright owners now have an unprecedented term of copyright protection (life plus seventy years) without the need to formally renew the copyright term. This fact is in stark contrast to the twenty-eight-year limitation on a copyright's duration prior to 1976, which held unless a copyright owner actually renewed the term of copyright with the Copyright Office. A leading presumption at that time was that a copyright owner would not go through the effort of renewal if he or she no longer perceived value in the work. Thus, the work would fall into the public domain so that everyone could freely use it. Unfortunately, many copyrights mistakenly fell into the public domain at that time if the owner did not act within the guidelines, with no way of regaining protection of an important work.

Now, because copyright owners have such a long term of copyright protection (life plus seventy years) without the need to formally renew the copyright term, contact information may also not be updated. Some argue that the "blessing" for owners is a "curse" for users who seek to build on copyrighted works or incorporate them, even legally, into their own.

Works that are difficult or impossible to link with their proper owners are called orphan works. In 2005, the Copyright Office conducted a study of orphan works and received hundreds of comments from individuals, organizations, libraries, archivists, and companies affected by the issue, including the National Writers Union/UAW 1981, the Authors Guild, and the Science Fiction and Fantasy Writers of America, Inc. The Copyright Office also hosted two public roundtable discussions on orphan works and several informal sessions to further vet the subject.

Members of the publishing industry came up with some creative solutions to the orphan-works problem. For example, the Science Fiction and Fantasy Writers of America suggested that the laws be changed (1) to require that prospective users conduct a reasonable investigation and properly attribute the work if possible; (2) to maintain a national registry separate from the Library of Congress where copyright owners list their work and status, and users post their intent to use; and (3) to maintain a national escrow fund to collect fees of fair-market value from users and hold those fees for a certain period of time (perhaps ten years or until claimed, if at all, by the copyright owner), after which the funds could be donated to charities.

The National Writers Union also supported a national registry and suggested a licensing agency, much like those in the music industry. On the other hand, the Authors Guild reached a different conclusion. It conducted a survey of its more than 2,100 members to find out how pervasive the problem is for authors and found that the overwhelming majority, 85 percent, reported that they had rarely or never been unable to locate a copyright owner. Therefore, the Authors Guild concluded that the problem may be dramatically overstated.

On March 8, 2006, Jule L. Sigall, Associate Register for Policy and International Affairs, testified before the Subcommittee on Courts, the Internet, and Intellectual Property, of the Committee on the Judiciary, to present the Copyright Office's findings and recommendations to address the orphan-works problem. Basically, the Copyright Office recommended that Congress amend the Copyright Act (1) to require users first to conduct a "reasonably diligent search for the owner" and thereafter, if unsuccessful, to use the work; (2) to attribute the work to the owner, if possible; and (3) if the owner resurfaces after use and sues the user for infringement, to limit the owner's damages to "reasonable compensation." Based on these findings and recommendations, new legislation was introduced in the House of Representatives on May 22, 2006, to address the problem of orphan works (see page 74).

9 Selling Your Rights and Getting Them Back

Any or all of the copyright owner's bundle of rights or any subdivision of those rights may be transferred to a third party. In other words, you may transfer one right in the bundle to one person or entity and another right or two or three to another person or entity. A transfer is defined in section 101 of the Copyright Act as an "assignment, mortgage, grant of an exclusive license, transfer by will or intestate succession, or any other change in the ownership of any or all of the exclusive rights in a copyright whether or not it is limited in time or place of effect."

How Copyrights Are Transferred

Generally, there are three types of transfers: (1) a nonexclusive license, under which you remain the owner of your work, and the licensee can use your work but cannot exclude others from doing so; (2) an exclusive license, under which you remain the owner of your work but no one other than the licensee can use the work—not even you; and (3) an assignment, under which you give ownership of your work to the transferee. Further limits on transfer include the number of rights transferred, the term, and the geographical scope. To be valid, the transfer of exclusive rights must be in a written agreement signed by the owner of the rights conveyed (or the owner's authorized agent). But nonexclusive transfer of a right does not require a written agreement. So for example, the transfer of the exclusive right of publication to a publisher or agent requires a signed agreement, but the transfer of the nonexclusive right to reproduce an excerpt of a literary work in a newsletter does not.

As a matter of course, however, you should get all agreements relating to your copyright interests in writing. Having a signed agreement memorializes the terms and reduces the likelihood of misunderstandings as to what was promised by each party.

A copyright may also be transferred by operation of law. For instance, copyright can be bequeathed by will or by state law if an individual dies without a will. Copyright is a personal property right, and it is subject to the various state laws and regulations that govern the ownership, inheritance, or transfer of personal property and the terms of contracts or conduct of business. For information about relevant state laws, consult an attorney in your area.

Copyright assignments can be filed, or recorded, in the Copyright Office as transfers of copyright ownership. Recording the assignment gives notice to the world that the copyright interest has been transferred. Although you are not required to record the transfer to make it valid, recording the assignment does provide certain legal advantages and may be required to validate the transfer against third parties. For instance, under certain conditions, recordation establishes the order of priority between conflicting transfers (that is, who received the transfer first), or between a conflicting transfer and a nonexclusive license. Recordation also establishes a public record of the transaction and provides "constructive notice," which is a legal term meaning that members of the public are deemed to have been notified even if they have not actually received notice of the transfer. To establish constructive notice, the recorded document must describe the work with specificity so that it could be identified by a reasonable search, and the work must be registered with the Copyright Office.

Reclaiming Your Copyright after Transfer

Did you know that regardless of the terms of your transfer document (e.g., a publishing agreement or a license), you have the right to reclaim your copyright? Discussion about this little-known legal right for authors is just starting to emerge in the publishing industry. Publishers, for instance, may not want authors to know that the "life of copyright" term in most publishing agreements can be rendered null and void if a statutory termination is properly effected. But because different versions of the copyright law apply to different works, depending on when they were created, registered, and transferred, and depending on who transferred the rights, there are different rules for terminating transfers of those works to third parties. I will examine pre-1978 transfers and those transfers made on or after January 1, 1978; but if you have a specific question regarding a potential transfer termination, please contact an intellectual property attorney who is well versed in literary law and transfer termination issues.

Pre-1978 Transfers

Due to several amendments to copyright law, pre-1978 works, governed by the Copyright Act of 1909, can be protected for up to ninety-five years. This includes the initial twenty-eight-year term of copyright (the initial term), plus the first twenty-eight-year renewal term (renewal term), plus an additional nineteen-year term (bonus term), and, thanks to Sonny Bono, the extended twenty-year term (extended bonus term). Through this series of statutory revisions, pre-1978 authors enjoy an additional sixty-seven years beyond the initial term of protection (provided the renewal was either affirmatively or automatically renewed).

But transfer rules do not hinge on the date of creation or registration per se but on the date the copyright was transferred. Section 304(c) of the Copyright Act allows a writer to reclaim his or her copyright if those rights were transferred (either by the writer or his or her heirs) before January 1, 1978. The window of opportunity to begin the transfer termination process begins either fifty-six years after the date the copyright was originally secured or on January 1, 1978, whichever is later. For pre-1978 transfers, writers actually have two opportunities to reclaim copyright; if the first opportunity fifty-six years after transfer passes, the second and final opportunity to recapture the last twenty years of copyright protection occurs seventy-five years after transfer. You must give at least two years but not more than ten years notice to the transferee that you intend to terminate the copyright transfer.

Post-1977 Transfers

Creators of works transferred on or after January 1, 1978, enjoy similar but not identical transfer termination rules. Section 203 of the Copyright Act provides that a transfer or license of copyright (or any right in the bundle of rights) executed by the author (but unlike a pre-1978 transfer *not* a transfer made by anyone other than the author) on or after January 1, 1978, is subject to termination under the following conditions:

❑ A single author who executed a grant may terminate it. If the author is deceased, then whoever is entitled to exercise more than one-half of that author's rights may terminate it.

❑ If two or more authors executed a grant of a joint work, a majority of the authors who executed it may terminate it. If any of the joint authors is dead, his or her termination interest may be exercised by whoever is entitled to exercise more than one-half of that author's interest.

This single, extremely valuable section of the Copyright Act, allowing for the reclaiming of rights by terminating transfers, empowers authors.

Note that the statutory termination provision does not apply to works made for hire or to transfers made by will. The termination right also does not apply to rights arising under foreign laws or derivative works. In the case of derivative works (for example, a movie based on a book), termination of the rights to the underlying work (the book) does not prevent the continued display and distribution of the derivative movie. Once the rights are terminated, however, no new derivative works can be created without permission of the author.

Not surprisingly, the rules to exercise the statutory termination right are specific and must be strictly adhered to or the right will be forever lost. In addition, the Copyright Office does not provide printed forms for the use of persons serving notices of termination.

First, termination can be effected only during a five-year window of opportunity. For works transferred on or after January 1, 1978, the window begins thirty-five years after the grant was made. Special rules apply if the right transferred is the right of publication. In that case, the window begins thirty-five years from the date of publication or at the end of forty years from the date the transfer was executed, whichever is earlier. Presumably this modification accounts for the gap in time between the date a publishing agreement is signed and the date the work is actually published.

Second, the original owner must deliver to the grantee a signed, written, advance termination notice, which includes the effective date of termination, not less than two years or more than ten years before the termination is to take effect. The notice must be signed by the original owner (or owners, as per the statute) or a duly authorized agent, who may be an attorney-in-fact under a power of attorney, or, if the original owner is deceased, an heir or beneficiary under a will. The notice must be recorded with the Copyright Office *before* the termination is to take place, and, of course, the underlying work must be registered with the Copyright Office.

Third, the Copyright Act states, "Termination of the grant may be effected *notwithstanding any agreement to the contrary . . .*" Therefore, you cannot "contract around" this right. In other words, you cannot waive these rights by contract. Your right to terminate exists until it is exercised or lost, pursuant to the terms of the statute.

Let's bring this topic home by way of example. Assume that Author, at age 30, signs a publishing agreement with XYZ Publisher on January 1, 2003. In that agreement, Author transfers to XYZ the right to publish in hardback and paperback and all subsidiary rights. The work is published eighteen months later, on July 1, 2004. On January 1, 2010, XYZ licenses the right to develop a motion picture based on the book.

Because the transferring contract was signed on January, 1, 2003, before the publication date, the five-year window springs into effect thirty-five years later, on January, 1, 2038, and ends on January 1, 2043. During that window, Author has the right to terminate the agreement and reclaim all rights transferred to Publisher. If Author intends to terminate the publishing agreement on the first date the window comes into effect, she will have to send a termination notice to Publisher or his assignee no earlier than January 1, 2028, and no later than January 1, 2036. Once the transfer terminates, Publisher can no longer create any derivative works or license that right to others.

It is crucial to understand when the termination window exists and to plan properly to reclaim your rights. Additionally, you should plan for the reclamation of your rights in your will so that your family, executor, or trustee knows that your intellectual property exists, and understands how to manage and protect those rights after your death. This, of course, means that you must consult a trust and estates attorney familiar with intellectual property laws to create an estate plan that includes a will and perhaps a trust, financial power of attorney, and healthcare power of attorney with a medical directive (aka a living will), so that you protect not only your personal property and real estate but also your intellectual property. In particular, consider creating a testamentary trust in your will to name a literary trustee knowledgeable about intellectual property to maintain and administer your intellectual property rights after your death. This is a special type of trustee who will probably be someone other than a person you would usually name because the literary trustee should be familiar with intellectual property law.

10 When Someone Violates Your Copyright

Copyright infringement is the violation of any of the rights in the bundle of rights explained in chapters 1 and 2—that is, the rights of reproduction, adaptation, distribution, public performance, and public display; the rights of attribution and integrity; and the right of importation. The Digital Millennium Copyright Act (DMCA), described in chapter 1, extended the existing Copyright Act to specifically address works on the Internet.

Determining Who Sues and Who Gets Sued

Generally speaking, the legal and beneficial owners of an exclusive right of copyright—which means the author, assignee, or exclusive licensee—have the right to sue for infringement, as long as the copyright is registered with the Copyright Office before initiating a lawsuit. But the holder of a nonexclusive right, such as a nonexclusive licensee, does not have the right to initiate an infringement suit. Limited exceptions apply in certain instances as, for example, when an individual assigns his or her copyright but retains the right to receive royalties.

Now that you know who can sue, you need to know who can be sued. There are four types of infringers, as the chart on the next page shows.

Type of Infringer	Description
Direct Infringer	One who actually uses copyrighted material without the consent of the copyright owner.
Contributory Infringer	One who substantially participates in the direct infringement of a copyright interest.
Vicarious Infringer	One who has the right and ability to supervise the actions of a direct infringer and has a financial stake in the infringing activity.
Criminal Infringer	One who infringes a copyright willfully either for the purpose of "commercial advantage or private financial gain," or by the reproduction or distribution of $1,000 worth of copies of copyrighted work during any 180-day period. A copyright owner must establish more than reproduction and distribution. She or he must also establish willful intent. And, in the case of felony infringement, the owner must establish that a copyright exists, that it was infringed by the defendant by reproduction and distribution of the copyrighted work, and that the defendant acted willfully, and copied or distributed at least ten copies at a value of more than $2,500 within a 180-day period.

Copyright Infringement Remedies

The Copyright Act provides four remedies for copyright infringement. Statutory damages are not available, however, if the infringement began before the work was registered, unless such registration is made *within three months after the first publication of the work.*

Injunctions: An injunction is a court declaration to stop the behavior giving rise to the lawsuit. For instance, a court may order an alleged infringer to stop making copies or to stop distributing the copyrighted work. Any court can, in its discretion, grant temporary and final injunctions "on such terms as it may deem reasonable to prevent or restrain infringement of a copyright."

Impounding Infringing Copies: When an infringement case is pending, the court has the discretion to impound all copies or phonorecords claimed to have been made or used in violation of the copyright owner's exclusive rights, and all plates, molds, matrices, masters, tapes, film negatives, or other articles by means of which such copies or phonorecords may be reproduced. If the plaintiff—the one who sues—in an infringement suit wins the case, the court can order the destruction of the copies and the methods of reproduction and distribution.

Damages and Profits: A plaintiff who wins an infringement lawsuit is entitled to either statutory damages or to actual damages and any additional profits of the infringer. If the work was registered within three months of publication, then statutory damages would be available; if not, then only actual damages would be available in addition to profits. To establish the infringer's profits, the copyright owner must present proof only of the infringer's gross revenue, and the infringer must prove his or her deductible expenses and the elements of profit attributable to factors other than the copyrighted work. If statutory damages are available, the plaintiff can recover for all infringements with respect to one work, an amount from $750 to $30,000, in the court's discretion.

In the case of willful infringement, the court has discretion to increase the damage award to a maximum of $150,000. If, however, the defendant establishes innocent infringement, the court can reduce the award to a minimum of $200.

 Statutory damages are awarded for each infringed work, not for each incidence of infringement. For example, if someone infringes the copyrighted work *When Pigs Fly* by making one hundred illegal copies, the copyright owner can recover between $200 and $150,000, not one hundred times that amount.

Costs and Attorney Fees: The court also has the discretion to award court costs and reasonable attorney fees to the prevailing party. The court considers a number of factors, namely, the losing party's frivolousness, motivation, and objective reasonableness, and the court's need to "advance considerations of compensation and deterrents."

Limitations on Actions

Criminal infringement cases must be filed within five years of the time the infringement took place, or the case is barred. Civil infringement actions must be filed within three years after the infringement occurred, or the right to sue is forfeited. These periods of time are commonly referred to as the statute of limitations because the law limits the amount of time during which you can sue.

11 Hot Topics in Copyright: Cases and Controversies

Part of the excitement of copyright law is the fact that it is dynamic, constantly changing and evolving. So I want to cover some of the topics actually being discussed and debated widely in the publishing and intellectual property worlds. I provide this information not to choose sides but to present the big picture so that you are informed about the controversies at issue. Remember: the discussions and debates of today often become the laws of tomorrow, and those laws affect your rights.

Google Print

In 2004, Google, the well-known Internet search engine, introduced Google Print, now known as Google Book Search. The company describes Google Book Search as a book marketing program that allows users of its search engine to preview a certain limited amount of a book's content and general information about the book in what Google calls a Snippet View. Of course, the copyright owner can increase the amount of content the user can view to a few pages or even to the entire book. Google Book Search also provides hyperlinks to various book retailers. It also collects advertising revenues, and shares search results and ad revenues with publishers. To display the content of books, Google secures permission from the publisher of the book—not the writer (unless the writer is self-published or otherwise controls electronic publication or display rights). Google is also working with libraries to include library collections in Google Book Search and show users information about the book plus a book's content in Snippet View.

Google asserts that its use of book content is permitted because copyright owners (in most cases the publishers) have to opt in, and that use of library books is fair use. But some writers are very concerned about possible copyright infringement of their works. And writer organizations like the Authors Guild are getting involved to ensure that participation by publishers and libraries in Google's program does not amount to rampant infringement of protected works. In fact, in 2005 the Authors Guild joined three other named plaintiffs in a lawsuit against Google, alleging that it engaged "in massive copyright infringement at the expense of the rights of individual writers." The Authors Guild reports at its Web site that Google entered into contracts with Stanford, Harvard, Oxford, the University of Michigan, and the New York Public Library "to create digital copies of substantial parts of their collections and to make those collections available for searching online" without the permission of the writers. The New York Public Library and Oxford, recognizing the potential infringement problems, are limiting the books scanned from their collections to those in the public domain. Not too long after the Authors Guild suit, the Association of American Publishers and five publishers filed a class-action suit against Google as well.

One problem of great concern to writers and publishers is the safety of their intellectual property. Google stresses that it hosts all information on its secure servers and that the copy, save, and paste functions on the user's browser are all disabled. But people who have tested this "security" have bragged in the blogosphere that they in fact are able to bypass these features with screen captures.

Another important issue is that publishing contracts may not give the author's consent for this use in some cases. Will writers challenge a publisher's use of works not permitted under the terms of their contracts? Keep an eye on this issue, because as the lawsuits move through the legal system only time will tell whether Google's precedent becomes the law of the land or whether those who create artistic and literary works, or own the rights to them, can successfully limit their use to those who are licensed and approved.

Tasini Freelancer Class-Action Settlement

After six freelance writers won the historic Supreme Court copyright infringement case *Tasini et al. v. New York Times*, against the *New York Times, Time Inc., Newsday,* and electronic database publishers LexisNexis and UMI, the Authors Guild sought to up the ante by pressing the publishers into a class-action lawsuit to collect money for all freelancers affected by the publishers' decision to use the freelancers' works in electronic format without permission. In the *Tasini* case (discussed more completely in chapter 12), the publishers argued that the grant of rights that referred to "print" also included the right to publish in electronic format based on their interpretation of the law.

On July 3, 2001, the Authors Guild on behalf of two of its members, Derrick Bell and Lynn Brenner, and an entire class of freelancers "similarly situated," filed a two-count class-action suit against the *New York Times* to collect monetary damages for past infringement and injunctive relief to prevent future infringement. The American

Society of Journalists and Authors (ASJA) also participated, and a similar National Writers Union (NWU) class action was ultimately joined to the Guild/ASJA suit.

Letty Cottin Pogrebin, then president of the Authors Guild, said that the Guild had "taken this action to protect the economic interests of our members and all freelance writers." The Guild also sought to counteract high-pressured publicity efforts by the *New York Times* to elicit support from the public by asserting that the *Times* would have to remove articles and pictures unless the freelancers granted the necessary permission to use copyrighted works. In articles posted at its Web site, the Guild expressed concern that the *Times* seemed to value the "loss" to the public more than it valued author rights.

On March 29, 2005, ASJA and NWU filed for approval an $18 million settlement agreement titled *In re Literary Works in Electronic Databases Copyright Litigation*. The court preliminarily approved the settlement on March 31, 2005. The settlement was amended because of certain sublicensing to Amazon.com and Highbeam Research, and then approved again on July 28, 2005, as amended. The final settlement was approved on September 27, 2005. The publisher defendants agreed to pay a minimum of $10 million and a maximum of $18 million to settle the lawsuit, to be applied to valid claims and all fees and expenses, all of which must be approved by the Court.

But in October 2005, an appeal was filed that postponed payment under the approved settlement agreement until information about class members could be clarified. The class-action Web site posted the following announcement about the current status: "On June 16, 2006, the Claims Administrator mailed out letters to class members who submitted claims, asking for further information, or advising that certain claims were ineligible." Therefore, an additional process to include or exclude certain members of the class must be completed before the settlement will be final and payments made. For additional information, visit the official class-action Web site at www.copyrightclass action.com and the plaintiff Web site at http://www.freelancerights.com.

Public Domain Enhancement Act of 2005

Representative Zoe Lofgren introduced HR 2408, the Public Domain Enhancement Act, to the House of Representatives on May 17, 2005, to allow abandoned copyrighted works to enter the public domain after fifty years. The bill defines an "abandoned work" as a work not renewed by paying a $1 fee fifty years after publication or by December 31, 2006, whichever occurs earlier, and then every ten years until term expires. The bill proposes that a form accompany each maintenance payment. The sponsor's rationale in support of the bill is that copyrighted material that is no longer commercially exploited should be released to the public domain so the public is not "unreasonably deprived of 'the fruits of an artist's labors.'" As of this writing, the bill is before the Subcommittee on Courts, the Internet, and Intellectual Property.

Orphan Works Act of 2006

The Orphan Works Act, HR 5439, was introduced in the House of Representatives on May 22, 2006, by Representative Lamar Smith from Texas. This bill seeks to limit the remedies available to copyright plaintiffs in cases in which, despite the due diligence on the part of the defendant to locate and contact the owner to seek permission and to attribute the copyrighted work to the owner (if possible), the copyright owner could not be located for purposes of securing permission. For purposes of this bill, due diligence would include, at a minimum, review of (1) the records of the Copyright Office that are relevant to identifying and locating copyright owners; (2) other sources of copyright ownership information reasonably available to users; (3) methods to identify copyright ownership information associated with a work; (4) sources of reasonably available technology tools and reasonably available expert assistance; and (5) best practices for documenting a reasonably diligent search. See page 59 for a complete discussion of the orphan-works problem and to find out what you can do to handle the situation when it is difficult or impossible to locate the copyright owner in order to get permission.

12 What Every Freelancer Should Know about Copyright

If you are a freelancer who submits an article, essay, poem, or other individual literary work to a collective work such as a magazine, newspaper, anthology, or Web site, then you need to understand your rights in your individual contribution *before* submitting your work—not after.

Contributing to a Collective Work

Copyright in your contribution to a collective work is completely separate and distinct from copyright in the collective work as a whole, and vests initially in you as the author of the contribution. And unless you expressly transfer the entire bundle of rights that makes up copyright or any of the individual rights in the bundle (see chapter 2), the copyright owner of the collective work is presumed to have acquired only the privilege of reproducing and distributing your contribution as part of that particular collective work, as well as any revision of that collective work, and any later collective work in the same series.

Of course, if you sign a contract that requires you to transfer some or all of your rights in your individual work to the publisher of the collective work, you should pay particular attention to whether the transfer is so comprehensive that it prevents even you from using your work for a certain period of time or forever. I cover these contractual issues in detail in my book *Contracts Companion for Writers*.

Know Your (Serial) Rights

When you transfer to a publisher the right to publish your work, you should spell out in writing exactly what rights the publisher has acquired. This doesn't need to be a formal document—a series of e-mails confirming the arrangement is certainly acceptable. But whatever the method of memorializing the deal, it should be clear whether the publisher is acquiring first serial rights, second serial rights (also known as reprint rights), all rights, or whether the publisher has commissioned you to create a work as a work made for hire to be used in a collective work. The following chart will help you distinguish among these various rights:

First serial rights	The publisher acquires the right to publish your unpublished work before anyone else does. Consider limiting this transfer by indicating a particular territory (North America) and language (English). Note: In publishing contracts, the terms "North America" and "South America" have specific meaning that differs from what you learned in geography class. In the contracts, sometimes "North America" includes Canada and sometimes it doesn't, so be sure to confirm whether the publisher intends to include Canada.
Second serial rights (aka reprint rights)	The publisher acquires the right to publish your work after the first serial publication.
Work made for hire	This means that the publisher—not you, the writer—owns the copyright. Try to avoid this if possible unless you receive adequate financial compensation. Work-made-for-hire agreements must be done *before* you begin working or else they are generally not valid because of the way copyright comes into existence (see chapters 2 and 5 for more information about copyright and work made for hire).
One-time rights	Sometimes a newspaper editor seeks one-time rights, meaning the right to publish your article once, regardless of whether that newspaper is first or second in line to publish.

Electronic Rights

Electronic rights are of particular concern to freelancers. The question of whether free-lance writers transferred electronics rights to publishers when they agreed to the initial "in print" form of publication was addressed in the now famous (or should I say infamous) *Tasini* case and its progeny. *Tasini* involved the *New York Times* and other publishers (*Newsday* and *Time*) and Jonathan Tasini on behalf of freelancers who transferred first serial print rights to the publishers. Those publishers licensed electronic rights of the freelance articles and photographs to searchable database publishers who allowed individual works to be accessed outside and apart from the magazines or newspapers that the works appeared in originally. The issue in the lawsuit was whether the print rights included electronic rights. The case worked its way up to the Supreme Court. That Court decided that in-print rights did not include electronic rights, and therefore the publisher had to secure those rights from the freelancer separately.

Other cases with similar facts involved National Geographic Society's use of freelance articles and photographs in a CD-ROM that allowed "in context" electronic searching, giving the look and feel of leafing through the pages of the printed magazine. Each of the prominent cases, *Greenberg* and *Faulkner*, came out with different decisions, so this issue may find its way to the Supreme Court as well.

A final case of interest is the *RosettaBooks* case, involving electronic books (e-books) and what constitutes a "book" in a publishing agreement. In the year 2000 and the beginning of 2001, RosettaBooks contracted with several authors to publish certain of their works—including *The Confessions of Nat Turner* and *Sophie's Choice* by William Styron; *Slaughterhouse Five, Breakfast of Champions, The Sirens of Titan, Cat's Cradle,* and *Player Piano* by Kurt Vonnegut; and *Promised Land* by Robert B. Parker—in digital format over the Internet. Random House had contracted with the authors twenty to forty years earlier to "print, publish and sell the work in book form."

The court held that "the most reasonable interpretation of the grant in the contracts at issue to 'print, publish and sell the work in book form'" does not include the right to publish the work as an e-book. At the outset, the phrase itself distinguishes between the pure content—in other words, "the work"—and the format of display—"in book form." This decision was upheld on appeal.

13 What Every Songwriter Should Know about Copyright

Until now, I have focused mostly on literary creations in the publishing industry (books, articles, magazines, and so forth). But copyright in a song (whether lyrics, music, or both) is created in the same way as in any other literary or artistic work (see chapter 2). And music copyright is made up of the same bundle of rights, which includes the right to publish.

What Music Publishing Is All About

Unless you are already a well-known songwriter, it will be a challenge to commercially exploit your music without the help of a music publisher, one who licenses your songs to others for flat fees or royalties so that your songs get recorded or played or synchronized in TV and film and so forth. Performance royalties are all right, but music publishing, if properly managed, is really where the money is in the music industry.

Music publishing can be big business. It is also confusing to many songwriters who tend to focus on the creative aspects of writing rather than the business and legal sides. Essentially, there are two potential income streams involved in songwriting: first is the songwriter's share as the creator and copyright owner, and second is the publisher's share for the person or company that actually enables the song to be released to the public (i.e., to be published). This has been explained in the past as the two "pies," where the total percentage of income is 200 percent (each of the pies equaling 100 percent). This explanation is somewhat outdated and only adds to confusion. Others explain the writer's share as 50 percent of the revenues and the publisher's share as the other 50 percent. Regardless of how you slice it (pun intended), in general, songwriters transfer some percentage (or all) of the copyright to the publisher, and keep the entire songwriter's share of income and none (or very little) of the publisher's share. The percentage of copyright transfers affects the way money is split between you and the publisher.

If you do a co-publishing deal in which you (or the publishing company that you form) team up with an established publisher, then you will most likely transfer 50 percent of the copyright to the publisher, keep the entire writer's share of revenues, and split the publisher's share of revenues fifty-fifty. Or you may be in a strong negotiating position and opt for an administration deal, in which case you will control copyright and keep all of the songwriter's share, all (or most) of the publisher's share, and simply pay to the company an administrative fee for handling the business of exploiting and managing your copyrights. Because this is a dramatically oversimplified explanation, please review the resources listed in Appendix A for books that cover this issue in greater depth.

How Songwriters and Publishers Get Paid

Songwriters make money from five basic income streams generated by royalties from the commercial exploitation of their songs via licensing: mechanical, performance, synchronization, print, and grand rights. It is also now common for songwriters to earn income from licensing samples. Sampling refers to taking a portion of an existing musical composition and using it as a musical element in a new song (a base line or hook, for example). Samples are most often used in hip hop and R&B, but they are becoming more widely used in other music genres as well.

Mechanical: The term "mechanical royalties" refers to the money collected by the publisher whenever a song is reproduced in any "per unit" format like a CD or cassette tape, for instance. The term originally referred to the mechanical reproduction of music by a device (literally pressing records, for those who remember those relics). There are negotiated licenses, in which price is determined by mutual agreement of the parties, and compulsory licenses based on what is called the statutory rate, an amount per unit set by copyright law. The current rate as of this writing is 8.5 cents per unit, and compulsory licenses are granted either by the Harry Fox Agency or the Copyright Office.

 NOTE: Music industry custom is to pay most songwriters (new and established) only 75% of the then current statutory rate for a maximum of 10 songs per album (regardless of how many additional songs are on the CD). So the formula with the current rate of 8.5 cents per song is 0.085 x .75 x 10, which yields a total mechanical income from one CD of only 64 cents.

Performance: Public performance royalties are generated every time a song is performed live or played on the radio, on television, in an elevator, in a nightclub, or even in a church. These royalties are tracked, collected, and paid directly to songwriters by organizations known as performing rights organizations: ASCAP, BMI, and SESAC, most notably. So publishers are not involved in collection of public performance royalties, but they are entitled to some percentage (usually 50 percent) of such, known as the publisher's share.

Synchronization: Synchronization refers to the process of linking a song (any part or all of it) with a visual image. For example, when a song is linked with a television commercial or movie, the user must license this right from the copyright holder. Synchronization deals (aka synch licenses or deals) have the potential to be very lucrative sources of revenue for publishers and songwriters, so special care should be taken when negotiating these rights. And generally, songwriters or publishers should enter into separate synch deals based on the opportunities presented. A related but separate license is a transcription license used by radio broadcasters to license songs for use in radio commercials.

Print: When songs are printed as sheet music (e.g., folios, song books, instruction books), a print license is required. The publisher issues print licenses and collects the royalties on behalf of the songwriter. Print-license royalties are not nearly as lucrative as other revenue streams, but they are still an important part of the entire publishing income.

Grand: The dramatic performance of songs involves licensing grand rights. Although grand rights are a lesser known licensing opportunity, their exploitation is another important licensing revenue stream. For example, an existing song may be used in a dramatic performance—say a musical or opera or ballet for which it was not expressly written. Use of that existing song in the dramatic performance requires permission, the grand rights license.

Managing Registrations—Early and Often

To successfully protect and exploit your songs, you must have a procedure in place to make sure that you register all of your songs (whether published or unpublished) and keep a record of all titles and registration numbers. While you may not have to register each song separately—in fact prolific writers may find it cost-prohibitive and unduly time-consuming to do so—you should register a bunch of songs at once and make this a regular practice. For example, once every quarter, review your catalog and submit all unregistered works in a collection titled "songs as of certain date" or "unpublished collection #1" and so forth, even if the songs will ultimately appear on different recordings or projects.

Being organized from the beginning and maintaining good records and timely registration (see page 22) is extremely important; it is what separates the mere artists in the red from the entrepreneurs in the black. Maintaining your registrations early and often will allow you to benefit from your creativity and maximize your value as a successful songwriter—both creatively and financially.

Appendix A Resources for Writers

Resource	Contact
Web Sites	
Copyright Clearance Center	www.copyright.**com**, not to be confused with copyright.**gov** (the official Copyright Office Web site listed below)
Copyright Office	www.copyright.gov
FindLaw.com: an online database of helpful legal resources on many different areas of the law	www.FindLaw.com
Publishing lawyer Lloyd Jassin	www.copylaw.com
Self-publishing guru Dan Poynter	www.parapublishing.com
Intellectual Property Owners Association	www.ipo.org
Internet Corporation for Assigned Names and Numbers (ICANN)	www.icann.org
Legal Information Institute of Cornell University	www.law.cornell.edu
Library of Congress	www.loc.gov
United States Patent and Trademark Office	www.uspto.gov

World Intellectual Property Organization (WIPO): an international organization focused on protecting the rights of intellectual property owners	www.wipo.org

Conferences

BookExpo America	www.bookexpoamerica.com
Frankfurt Book Fair	www.frankfurt-bookfair.com
Harlem Book Fair	www.qbr.com
Horror Writers Association Annual Conference	www.horror.org
Infinity Publishing	www.authorsconference.com
Latino Book & Family Festival	www.latinobookfestival.com
Maui Writers Conference	www.mauiwriters.com
Romance Writers Association Annual Conference	www.rwanational.org
Shaw Guides: perhaps the most comprehensive listing of conferences available on the Internet	writing.shawguides.com
Writers Conference at Penn	http://www.sas.upenn.edu/CGS/cultural /writersconf/index.php

Organizations

American Society of Journalists and Authors	www.asja.org
Association of Authors and Publishers	www.authorsandpublishers.org
The Authors Guild	www.authorsguild.org

National Association of Women Writers	www.naww.org
National Writers Union	www.nwu.org
Publishers Marketing Association (PMA)	www.pma-online.org
Small Publishers, Artists, and Writers Network (SPAWN)	www.spawn.org
Small Publishers Association of North America (SPAN)	www.spannet.org
Society of Children's Book Writers and Illustrators (SCBWI)	www.scbwi.org
Women's National Book Association	www.wnba-books.org
Writer's Guild of America	www.wga.org (west coast) www.wga-east.org (east coast)

Magazines

Black Issues Book Review	www.bibookreview.com
Foreword Magazine	www.forewordmagazine.net
Poets and Writers	www.pw.org
Publishers Weekly	www.publishersweekly.com
Quarterly Black Review	www.qbr.com
The Writer	www.thewritermagazine.com
Writer's Digest	www.writersdigest.com

Books

This Business of Music	M. William Krasilovsky, et al.

All You Need to Know about the Music Business	Donald S. Passman
The Plain and Simple Guide to Music Publishing	Randall Wixen
The Self-Publishing Manual: How to Write, Print, and Sell Your Own Book	Dan Poynter
Complete Guide to Self-Publishing: Everything You Need to Know to Write, Publish, Promote, and Sell Your Own Book	Tom and Marilyn Ross
The Publishing Game	Fern Reiss

Appendix B Forms

Form TX

Detach and read these instructions before completing this form.
Make sure all applicable spaces have been filled in before you return this form.

BASIC INFORMATION

When to Use This Form: Use Form TX for registration of published or unpublished nondramatic literary works, excluding periodicals or serial issues. This class includes a wide variety of works: fiction, nonfiction, poetry, textbooks, reference works, directories, catalogs, advertising copy, compilations of information, and computer programs. For periodicals and serials, use Form SE.

Deposit to Accompany Application: An application for copyright registration must be accompanied by a deposit consisting of copies or phonorecords representing the entire work for which registration is to be made. The following are the general deposit requirements as set forth in the statute:

Unpublished Work: Deposit one complete copy (or phonorecord)

Published Work: Deposit two complete copies (or one phonorecord) of the best edition.

Work First Published Outside the United States: Deposit one complete copy (or phonorecord) of the first foreign edition.

Contribution to a Collective Work: Deposit one complete copy (or phonorecord) of the best edition of the collective work.

The Copyright Notice: Before March 1, 1989, the use of copyright notice was mandatory on all published works, and any work first published before that date should have carried a notice. For works first published on and after March 1, 1989, use of the copyright notice is optional. For more information about copyright notice, see Circular 3, *Copyright Notices.*

For Further Information: To speak to a Copyright Office staff member, call (202) 707-3000 (TTY: (202) 707-6737). Recorded information is available 24 hours a day. Order forms and other publications from the address in space 9 or call the Forms and Publications Hotline at (202) 707-9100. Access and download circulars, forms, and other information from the Copyright Office website at *www.copyright.gov.*

LINE-BY-LINE INSTRUCTIONS

Please type or print using black ink. The form is used to produce the certificate.

1 SPACE 1: Title

Title of This Work: Every work submitted for copyright registration must be given a title to identify that particular work. If the copies or phonorecords of the work bear a title or an identifying phrase that could serve as a title, transcribe that wording *completely* and *exactly* on the application. Indexing of the registration and future identification of the work will depend on the information you give here.

Previous or Alternative Titles: Complete this space if there are any additional titles for the work under which someone searching for the registration might be likely to look or under which a document pertaining to the work might be recorded.

Publication as a Contribution: If the work being registered is a contribution to a periodical, serial, or collection, give the title of the contribution in the "Title of This Work" space. Then, in the line headed "Publication as a Contribution," give information about the collective work in which the contribution appeared.

2 SPACE 2: Author(s)

General Instructions: After reading these instructions, decide who are the "authors" of this work for copyright purposes. Then, unless the work is a "collective work," give the requested information about every "author" who contributed any appreciable amount of copyrightable matter to this version of the work. If you need further space, request Continuation Sheets. In the case of a collective work, such as an anthology, collection of essays, or encyclopedia, give information about the author of the collective work as a whole.

Name of Author: The fullest form of the author's name should be given. Unless the work was "made for hire," the individual who actually created the work is its "author." In the case of a work made for hire, the statute provides that "the employer or other person for whom the work was prepared is considered the author."

What Is a "Work Made for Hire"? A "work made for hire" is defined as (1) "a work prepared by an employee within the scope of his or her employment"; or (2) "a work specially ordered or commissioned for use as a contribution to a collective work, as a part of a motion picture or other audiovisual work, as a translation, as a supplementary work, as a compilation, as an instructional text, as a test, as answer material for a test, or as an atlas, if the parties expressly agree in a written instrument signed by them that the works shall be considered a work made for hire." If you have checked "Yes" to indicate that the work was "made for hire," you must give the full legal name of the employer (or other person for whom the work was prepared). You may also include the name of the employee along with the name of the employer (for example: "Elster Publishing Co., employer for hire of John Ferguson").

"Anonymous" or "Pseudonymous" Work: An author's contribution to a work is "anonymous" if that author is not identified on the copies or phonorecords of the work. An author's contribution to a work is "pseudonymous" if that author is identified on the copies or phonorecords under a fictitious name. If the work is "anonymous" you may: (1) leave the line blank; or (2) state "anonymous" on the line; or (3) reveal the author's identity. If the work is "pseudonymous" you may: (1) leave the line blank; or (2) give the pseudonym and identify it as such (for example: "Huntley Haverstock, pseudonym"); or (3) reveal the author's name, making clear which is the real name and which is the pseudonym (for example, "Judith Barton, whose pseudonym is Madeline Elster"). However, the citizenship or domicile of the author *must* be given in all cases.

Dates of Birth and Death: If the author is dead, the statute requires that the year of death be included in the application unless the work is anonymous or pseudonymous. The author's birth date is optional but is useful as a form of identification. Leave this space blank if the author's contribution was a "work made for hire."

Form TX

Author's Nationality or Domicile: Give the country of which the author is a citizen or the country in which the author is domiciled. Nationality or domicile *must* be given in all cases.

Nature of Authorship: After the words "Nature of Authorship," give a brief general statement of the nature of this particular author's contribution to the work. Examples: "Entire text"; "Coauthor of entire text"; "Computer program"; "Editorial revisions"; "Compilation and English translation"; "New text."

3 SPACE 3: Creation and Publication

General Instructions: Do not confuse "creation" with "publication." Every application for copyright registration must state "the year in which creation of the work was completed." Give the date and nation of first publication only if the work has been published.

Creation: Under the statute, a work is "created" when it is fixed in a copy or phonorecord for the first time. Where a work has been prepared over a period of time, the part of the work existing in fixed form on a particular date constitutes the created work on that date. The date you give here should be the year in which the author completed the particular version for which registration is now being sought, even if other versions exist or if further changes or additions are planned.

Publication: The statute defines "publication" as "the distribution of copies or phonorecords of a work to the public by sale or other transfer of ownership, or by rental, lease, or lending." A work is also "published" if there has been an "offering to distribute copies or phonorecords to a group of persons for purposes of further distribution, public performance, or public display." Give the full date (month, day, year) when, and the country where, publication first occurred. If first publication took place simultaneously in the United States and other countries, it is sufficient to state "U.S.A."

4 SPACE 4: Claimant(s)

Name(s) and Address(es) of Copyright Claimant(s): Give the name(s) and address(es) of the copyright claimant(s) in this work even if the claimant is the same as the author. Copyright in a work belongs initially to the author of the work (including, in the case of a work made for hire, the employer or other person for whom the work was prepared). The copyright claimant is either the author of the work or a person or organization to whom the copyright initially belonging to the author has been transferred.

Transfer: The statute provides that, if the copyright claimant is not the author, the application for registration must contain "a brief statement of how the claimant obtained ownership of the copyright." If any copyright claimant named in space 4 is not an author named in space 2, give a brief statement explaining how the claimant(s) obtained ownership of the copyright. Examples: "By written contract"; "Transfer of all rights by author"; "Assignment"; "By will." Do not attach transfer documents or other attachments or riders.

5 SPACE 5: Previous Registration

General Instructions: The questions in space 5 are intended to show whether an earlier registration has been made for this work and, if so, whether there is any basis for a new registration. As a general rule, only one basic copyright registration can be made for the same version of a particular work.

Same Version: If this version is substantially the same as the work covered by a previous registration, a second registration is not generally possible unless: (1) the work has been registered in unpublished form and a second registration is now being sought to cover this first published edition; or (2) someone other than the author is identified as copyright claimant in the earlier registration, and the author is now seeking registration in his or her own name. If either of these two exceptions applies, check the appropriate box and give the earlier registration number and date. Otherwise, do not submit Form TX. Instead, write the Copyright Office for information about supplementary registration or recordation of transfers of copyright ownership.

Changed Version: If the work has been changed and you are now seeking registration to cover the additions or revisions, check the last box in space 5, give the earlier registration number and date, and complete both parts of space 6 in accordance with the instructions below.

Previous Registration Number and Date: If more than one previous registration has been made for the work, give the number and date of the latest registration.

6 SPACE 6: Derivative Work or Compilation

General Instructions: Complete space 6 if this work is a "changed version," "compilation," or "derivative work" and if it incorporates one or more earlier works that have already been published or registered for copyright or that have fallen into the public domain. A "compilation" is defined as "a work formed by the collection and assembling of preexisting materials or of data that are selected, coordinated, or arranged in such a way that the resulting work as a whole constitutes an original work of authorship." A "derivative work" is "a work based on one or more preexisting works." Examples of derivative works include translations, fictionalizations, abridgments, condensations, or "any other form in which a work may be recast, transformed, or adapted." Derivative works also include works "consisting of editorial revisions, annotations, or other modifications" if these changes, as a whole, represent an original work of authorship.

Preexisting Material (space 6a): For derivative works, complete this space *and* space 6b. In space 6a identify the preexisting work that has been recast, transformed, or adapted. The preexisting work may be material that has been previously published, previously registered, or that is in the public domain. An example of preexisting material might be: "Russian version of Goncharov's 'Oblomov.'"

Material Added to This Work (space 6b): Give a brief, general statement of the new material covered by the copyright claim for which registration is sought. *Derivative work* examples include: "Foreword, editing, critical annotations"; "Translation"; "Chapters 11–17." If the work is a *compilation*, describe both the compilation itself and the material that has been compiled. Example: "Compilation of certain 1917 speeches by Woodrow Wilson." A work may be both a derivative work and compilation, in which case a sample statement might be: "Compilation and additional new material."

7, 8, 9 SPACE 7, 8, 9: Fee, Correspondence, Certification, Return Address

Deposit Account: If you maintain a Deposit Account in the Copyright Office, identify it in space 7a. Otherwise leave the space blank and send the fee with your application and deposit.

Correspondence (space 7b): Give the name, address, area code, telephone number, fax number, and email address (if available) of the person to be consulted if correspondence about this application becomes necessary.

Certification (space 8): The application cannot be accepted unless it bears the date and the *handwritten signature* of the author or other copyright claimant, or of the owner of exclusive right(s), or of the duly authorized agent of author, claimant, or owner of exclusive right(s).

Address for Return of Certificate (space 9): The address box must be completed legibly since the certificate will be returned in a window envelope.

Form TX   Page 3 of 4

Copyright Office fees are subject to change.
For current fees, check the Copyright Office
website at *www.copyright.gov*, write the Copyright Office, or call (202) 707-3000.

Ⓒ Form TX
For a Nondramatic Literary Work
UNITED STATES COPYRIGHT OFFICE

REGISTRATION NUMBER

_____
TX   TXU
EFFECTIVE DATE OF REGISTRATION

_____
Month   Day   Year

DO NOT WRITE ABOVE THIS LINE. IF YOU NEED MORE SPACE, USE A SEPARATE CONTINUATION SHEET.

1   **TITLE OF THIS WORK ▼**

PREVIOUS OR ALTERNATIVE TITLES ▼

PUBLICATION AS A CONTRIBUTION If this work was published as a contribution to a periodical, serial, or collection, give information about the collective work in which the contribution appeared.   **Title of Collective Work ▼**

If published in a periodical or serial give: Volume ▼   Number ▼   Issue Date ▼   On Pages ▼

2 a   **NAME OF AUTHOR ▼**   **DATES OF BIRTH AND DEATH**
Year Born ▼   Year Died ▼

Was this contribution to the work a "work made for hire"?   **AUTHOR'S NATIONALITY OR DOMICILE**   Name of Country
☐ Yes   OR { Citizen of ▶ _____
☐ No   { Domiciled in▶ _____

WAS THIS AUTHOR'S CONTRIBUTION TO THE WORK
Anonymous?   ☐ Yes ☐ No
Pseudonymous?   ☐ Yes ☐ No
If the answer to either of these questions is "Yes," see detailed instructions.

NATURE OF AUTHORSHIP Briefly describe nature of material created by this author in which copyright is claimed. ▼

NOTE

Under the law, the "author" of a "work made for hire" is generally the employer, not the employee (see instructions). For any part of this work that was "made for hire" check "Yes" in the space provided, give the employer (or other person for whom the work was prepared) as "Author" of that part, and leave the space for dates of birth and death blank.

b   **NAME OF AUTHOR ▼**   **DATES OF BIRTH AND DEATH**
Year Born ▼   Year Died ▼

Was this contribution to the work a "work made for hire"?   **AUTHOR'S NATIONALITY OR DOMICILE**   Name of Country
☐ Yes   OR { Citizen of ▶ _____
☐ No   { Domiciled in▶ _____

WAS THIS AUTHOR'S CONTRIBUTION TO THE WORK
Anonymous?   ☐ Yes ☐ No
Pseudonymous?   ☐ Yes ☐ No
If the answer to either of these questions is "Yes," see detailed instructions.

NATURE OF AUTHORSHIP Briefly describe nature of material created by this author in which copyright is claimed. ▼

c   **NAME OF AUTHOR ▼**   **DATES OF BIRTH AND DEATH**
Year Born ▼   Year Died ▼

Was this contribution to the work a "work made for hire"?   **AUTHOR'S NATIONALITY OR DOMICILE**   Name of Country
☐ Yes   OR { Citizen of ▶ _____
☐ No   { Domiciled in▶ _____

WAS THIS AUTHOR'S CONTRIBUTION TO THE WORK
Anonymous?   ☐ Yes ☐ No
Pseudonymous?   ☐ Yes ☐ No
If the answer to either of these questions is "Yes," see detailed instructions.

NATURE OF AUTHORSHIP Briefly describe nature of material created by this author in which copyright is claimed. ▼

3 a   **YEAR IN WHICH CREATION OF THIS WORK WAS COMPLETED**   This information must be given in all cases.   ◀Year   **b** **DATE AND NATION OF FIRST PUBLICATION OF THIS PARTICULAR WORK**   Complete this information ONLY if this work has been published.   Month ▶ _____ Day▶ _____ Year▶ _____   ◀ Nation

4   **COPYRIGHT CLAIMANT(S)** Name and address must be given even if the claimant is the same as the author given in space 2. ▼

See instructions before completing this space.

TRANSFER If the claimant(s) named here in space 4 is (are) different from the author(s) named in space 2, give a brief statement of how the claimant(s) obtained ownership of the copyright. ▼

DO NOT WRITE HERE   OFFICE USE ONLY
APPLICATION RECEIVED
_____
ONE DEPOSIT RECEIVED
_____
TWO DEPOSITS RECEIVED
_____
FUNDS RECEIVED

MORE ON BACK ▶   • Complete all applicable spaces (numbers 5-9) on the reverse side of this page.
• See detailed instructions.   • Sign the form at line 8.

DO NOT WRITE HERE
Page 1 of _____ pages

Form TX   Page 4 of 4

<table>
<tr><td>EXAMINED BY</td><td rowspan="2">FORM TX</td></tr>
<tr><td>CHECKED BY</td></tr>
<tr><td>☐ CORRESPONDENCE
Yes</td><td>FOR
COPYRIGHT
OFFICE
USE
ONLY</td></tr>
</table>

DO NOT WRITE ABOVE THIS LINE. IF YOU NEED MORE SPACE, USE A SEPARATE CONTINUATION SHEET.

PREVIOUS REGISTRATION Has registration for this work, or for an earlier version of this work, already been made in the Copyright Office?

☐ Yes ☐ No If your answer is "Yes," why is another registration being sought? (Check appropriate box.) ▼

a. ☐ This is the first published edition of a work previously registered in unpublished form.

b. ☐ This is the first application submitted by this author as copyright claimant.

c. ☐ This is a changed version of the work, as shown by space 6 on this application.

If your answer is "Yes," give: **Previous Registration Number** ▶   Year of Registration ▶

5

DERIVATIVE WORK OR COMPILATION

Preexisting Material Identify any preexisting work or works that this work is based on or incorporates. ▼

a

6

See instructions before completing this space.

Material Added to This Work Give a brief, general statement of the material that has been added to this work and in which copyright is claimed. ▼

b

DEPOSIT ACCOUNT If the registration fee is to be charged to a Deposit Account established in the Copyright Office, give name and number of Account.

Name ▼   **Account Number** ▼

a

7

CORRESPONDENCE Give name and address to which correspondence about this application should be sent.   Name/Address/Apt/City/State/Zip ▼

b

Area code and daytime telephone number ▶   Fax number ▶

Email ▶

CERTIFICATION* I, the undersigned, hereby certify that I am the

Check only one ▶ {
☐ author
☐ other copyright claimant
☐ owner of exclusive right(s)
☐ authorized agent of _____
}

of the work identified in this application and that the statements made by me in this application are correct to the best of my knowledge.

Name of author or other copyright claimant, or owner of exclusive right(s) ▲

8

Typed or printed name and date ▼ If this application gives a date of publication in space 3, do not sign and submit it before that date.

Date ▶ _____

Handwritten signature (X) ▼

X _____

Certificate will be mailed in window envelope to this address:

Name ▼

Number/Street/Apt ▼

City/State/ZIP ▼

YOU MUST:
· Complete all necessary spaces
· Sign your application in space 8

SEND ALL 3 ELEMENTS IN THE SAME PACKAGE:
1. Application form
2. Nonrefundable filing fee in check or money order payable to *Register of Copyrights*
3. Deposit material

MAIL TO:
Library of Congress
Copyright Office
101 Independence Avenue SE
Washington, DC 20559-6222

9

Form TX – Full Rev: 07/2006 Print: 07/2006 – 30,000 Printed on recycled paper

U.S. Government Printing Office: 2004-320-958/60,122

Instructions for Short Form TX

For nondramatic literary works, including fiction and nonfiction, books, short stories, poems, collections of poetry, essays, articles in serials, and computer programs

USE THIS FORM IF—

1. You are the *only* author and copyright owner of this work, *and*
2. The work was *not* made for hire, *and*
3. The work is completely new (does not contain a substantial amount of material that has been previously published or registered or is in the public domain).

If any of the above does not apply, you must use standard Form TX.
Note: *Short Form TX is not appropriate for an anonymous author who does not wish to reveal his or her identity.*

HOW TO COMPLETE SHORT FORM TX

- Type or print in black ink.
- Be clear and legible. (Your certificate of registration will be copied from your form.)
- Give only the information requested.

Note: You may use a continuation sheet (Form __/CON) to list individual titles in a collection. Complete Space A and list the individual titles under Space C on the back page. Space B is not applicable to short forms.

1 Title of This Work

You must give a title. If there is no title, state "UNTITLED." If you are registering an unpublished collection, give the collection title you want to appear in our records (for example: "Joan's Poems, Volume 1"). Alternative title: If the work is known by two titles, you also may give the second title. If the work has been published as part of a larger work (including a periodical), give the title of that larger work in addition to the title of the contribution.

2 Name and Address of Author and Owner of the Copyright

Give your name and mailing address. You may include your pseudonym followed by "pseud." Also, give the nation of which you are a citizen or where you have your domicile (i.e., permanent residence).
Give daytime phone and fax numbers and email address, if available.

3 Year of Creation

Give the latest year in which you completed the work you are registering at this time. A work is "created" when it is written down, stored in a computer, or otherwise "fixed" in a tangible form.

4 Publication

If the work has been published (i.e., if copies have been distributed to the public), give the complete date of publication (month, day, and year) and the nation where the publication first took place.

5 Type of Authorship in This Work

Check the box or boxes that describe your authorship in the copy you are sending with the application. For example, if you are registering a story and are planning to add illustrations later, check only the box for "text."

A "compilation" of terms or of data is a selection, coordination, or arrangement of such information into a chart, directory, or other form. A compilation of previously published or public domain material must be registered using a standard Form TX.

6 Signature of Author

Sign the application in black ink and check the appropriate box. The person signing the application should be the author or his/her authorized agent.

7 Person to Contact for Rights and Permissions

This space is optional. You may give the name and address of the person or organization to contact for permission to use the work. You may also provide phone, fax, or email information.

8 Certificate Will Be Mailed

This space must be completed. Your certificate of registration will be mailed in a window envelope to this address. Also, if the Copyright Office needs to contact you, we will write to this address.

9 Deposit Account

Complete this space only if you currently maintain a deposit account in the Copyright Office.

▓ MAIL WITH THE FORM ▓

- The filing fee in the form of a check or money order (*no cash*) payable to *Register of Copyrights*, and
- One or two copies of the work. If the work is unpublished, send one copy. If published, send two copies of the best published edition. (If first published outside the U.S., send one copy either as first published or of the best edition.) **Note:** Inquire about special requirements for works first published before 1978. Copies submitted become the property of the U.S. Government.

Mail everything (application form, copy or copies, and fee) *in one package* to:
Library of Congress
Copyright Office
101 Independence Avenue SE
Washington, DC 20559-6000

QUESTIONS? Call (202) 707-3000 [TTY: (202) 707-6737] between 8:30 a.m. and 5:00 p.m. eastern time, Monday through Friday except federal holidays. For forms and informational circulars, call (202) 707-9100 24 hours a day, 7 days a week, or download them from the Copyright Office website at *www.copyright.gov.*

Form TX (Short Form)

Copyright Office fees are subject to change.
For current fees, check the Copyright Office
website at *www.copyright.gov*, write the Copyright Office, or call (202) 707-3000.

Ⓒ Short Form TX
For a Nondramatic Literary Work
UNITED STATES COPYRIGHT OFFICE

REGISTRATION NUMBER

TX _____ TXU _____

Effective Date of Registration

Application Received

Deposit Received
One _____ | Two _____

Examined By

Correspondence ☐

Fee Received

TYPE OR PRINT IN BLACK INK. DO NOT WRITE ABOVE THIS LINE.

1 **Title of This Work:**

Alternative title or title of larger work in which this work was published:

2 **Name and Address of Author and Owner of the Copyright:**

Nationality or domicile:
Phone, fax, and email:

Phone ( ) _____ Fax ( ) _____
Email

3 **Year of Creation:**

4 **If work has been published, Date and Nation of Publication:**

a. Date _____ _____ _____
         Month   Day   Year

(Month, day, and year all required)

b. Nation

5 **Type of Authorship in This Work:**

Check all that this author created.

☐ Text (includes fiction, nonfiction, poetry, computer programs, etc.)
☐ Illustrations
☐ Photographs
☐ Compilation of terms or data

6 **Signature:**

Registration cannot be completed without a signature.

I certify that the statements made by me in this application are correct to the best of my knowledge. Check one:

☐ Author ☐ Authorized agent

X _____

7 **Name and Address of Person to Contact for Rights and Permissions:**

Phone, fax, and email:

OPTIONAL

☐ Check here if same as #2 above.

Phone ( ) _____ Fax ( ) _____
Email

8 Certificate will be mailed in window envelope to this address:

Name ▼

Number/Street/Apt ▼

City/State/Zip ▼

Complete this space only if you currently hold a Deposit Account in the Copyright Office.

9 Deposit Account #_____
Name _____
_____
_____
_____

DO NOT WRITE HERE   Page 1 of _____ pages

Form TX-Short Rev: 07/2006 Print: 07/2006—30,000 Printed on recycled paper   U.S. Government Printing Office: 2004-320-958/60,124

Form PA

Detach and read these instructions before completing this form.
Make sure all applicable spaces have been filled in before you return this form.

━━━━━━━━━━━━━━━━ **BASIC INFORMATION** ━━━━━━━━━━━━━━━━

When to Use This Form: Use Form PA for registration of published or unpublished works of the performing arts. This class includes works prepared for the purpose of being "performed" directly before an audience or indirectly "by means of any device or process." Works of the performing arts include: (1) musical works, including any accompanying words; (2) dramatic works, including any accompanying music; (3) pantomimes and choreographic works; and (4) motion pictures and other audiovisual works.

Deposit to Accompany Application: An application for copyright registration must be accompanied by a deposit consisting of copies or phonorecords representing the entire work for which registration is made. The following are the general deposit requirements as set forth in the statute:

Unpublished Work: Deposit one complete copy (or phonorecord).

Published Work: Deposit two complete copies (or one phonorecord) of the best edition.

Work First Published Outside the United States: Deposit one complete copy (or phonorecord) of the first foreign edition.

Contribution to a Collective Work: Deposit one complete copy (or phonorecord) of the best edition of the collective work.

Motion Pictures: Deposit *both* of the following: (1) a separate written description of the contents of the motion picture; and (2) for a published work, one complete copy of the best edition of the motion picture; or, for an unpublished work, one complete copy of the motion picture or identifying material. Identifying material may be either an audiorecording of

the entire soundtrack or one frame enlargement or similar visual print from each 10-minute segment.

The Copyright Notice: Before March 1, 1989, the use of copyright notice was mandatory on all published works, and any work first published before that date should have carried a notice. For works first published on and after March 1, 1989, use of the copyright notice is optional. For more information about copyright notice, see Circular 3, *Copyright Notice.*

For Further Information: To speak to a Copyright Office staff member, call (202) 707-3000 (TTY: (202) 707-6737). Recorded information is available 24 hours a day. Order forms and other publications from the address in space 9 or call the Forms and Publications Hotline at (202) 707-9100. Access and download circulars, forms, and other information from the Copyright Office website at *www.copyright.gov.*

━━━━━━━━━━━━━━━━ **LINE-BY-LINE INSTRUCTIONS** ━━━━━━━━━━━━━━━━

Please type or print using black ink. The form is used to produce the certificate.

1 ## SPACE 1: Title

Title of This Work: Every work submitted for copyright registration must be given a title to identify that particular work. If the copies or phonorecords of the work bear a title (or an identifying phrase that could serve as a title), transcribe that wording *completely* and *exactly* on the application. Indexing of the registration and future identification of the work will depend on the information you give here. If the work you are registering is an entire "collective work" (such as a collection of plays or songs), give the overall title of the collection. If you are registering one or more individual contributions to a collective work, give the title of each contribution, followed by the title of the collection. For an unpublished collection, you may give the titles of the individual works after the collection title.

Previous or Alternative Titles: Complete this space if there are any additional titles for the work under which someone searching for the registration might be likely to look, or under which a document pertaining to the work might be recorded.

Nature of This Work: Briefly describe the general nature or character of the work being registered for copyright. Examples: "Music"; "Song Lyrics"; "Words and Music"; "Drama"; "Musical Play"; "Choreography"; "Pantomime"; "Motion Picture"; "Audiovisual Work."

2 ## SPACE 2: Author(s)

General Instructions: After reading these instructions, decide who are the "authors" of this work for copyright purposes. Then, unless the work is a "collective work," give the requested information about every "author" who contributed any appreciable amount of copyrightable matter to this version of the work. If you need further space, request additional Continuation Sheets. In the case of a collective work such as a songbook or a collection of plays, give information about the author of the collective work as a whole.

Name of Author: The fullest form of the author's name should be given. Unless the work was "made for hire," the individual who actually created the work is its "author." In the case of a work made for hire, the statute provides that "the employer or other person for whom the work was prepared is considered the author."

What Is a "Work Made for Hire"? A "work made for hire" is defined as: (1) "a work prepared by an employee within the scope of his or her employment"; or (2) "a work specially ordered or commissioned for use as a contribution to a collective work, as a part of a motion picture or other audiovisual work, as a translation, as a supplementary work, as a compilation, as an instructional text, as a test, as answer material for a test, or as an atlas, if the parties expressly agree in a written instrument signed by them that the work shall be considered a work made for hire." If you have checked "Yes" to indicate that the work was "made for hire," you must give the full legal name of the employer (or other person for whom the work was prepared). You may also include the name of the employee along with the name of the employer (for example: "Elster Music Co., employer for hire of John Ferguson").

"Anonymous" or "Pseudonymous" Work: An author's contribution to a work is "anonymous" if that author is not identified on the copies or phonorecords of the work. An author's contribution to a work is "pseudonymous" if that author is identified on the copies or phonorecords under a fictitious name. If the work is "anonymous" you may: (1) leave the line blank; or (2) state "anonymous" on the line; or (3) reveal the author's identity. If the work is "pseudonymous" you may: (1) leave the line blank; or (2) give the pseudonym and identify it as such (example: "Huntley Haverstock, pseudonym"); or (3) reveal the author's name, making clear which is the real name and which is the pseudonym (for example: "Judith Barton, whose pseudonym is Madeline Elster). However, the citizenship or domicile of the author *must* be given in all cases.

Dates of Birth and Death: If the author is dead, the statute requires that the year of death be included in the application unless the work is anonymous or pseudonymous. The author's birth date is optional, but is useful as a form of identification. Leave this space blank if the author's contribution was a "work made for hire."

Author's Nationality or Domicile: Give the country of which the author is a citizen, or the country in which the author is domiciled. Nationality or domicile *must* be given in all cases.

Nature of Authorship: Give a brief general statement of the nature of this particular author's contribution to the work. Examples: "Words"; "Coauthor of Music"; "Words and Music"; "Arrangement"; "Coauthor of Book and Lyrics"; "Dramatization"; "Screen Play"; "Compilation and English Translation"; "Editorial Revisions."

3 SPACE 3: Creation and Publication

General Instructions: Do not confuse "creation" with "publication." Every application for copyright registration must state "the year in which creation of the work was completed." Give the date and nation of first publication only if the work has been published.

Creation: Under the statute, a work is "created" when it is fixed in a copy or phonorecord for the first time. Where a work has been prepared over a period of time, the part of the work existing in fixed form on a particular date constitutes the created work on that date. The date you give here should be the year in which the author completed the particular version for which registration is now being sought, even if other versions exist or if further changes or additions are planned.

Publication: The statute defines "publication" as "the distribution of copies or phonorecords of a work to the public by sale or other transfer of ownership, or by rental, lease, or lending"; a work is also "published" if there has been an "offering to distribute copies or phonorecords to a group of persons for purposes of further distribution, public performance, or public display." Give the full date (month, day, year) when, and the country where, publication first occurred. If first publication took place simultaneously in the United States and other countries, it is sufficient to state "U.S.A."

4 SPACE 4: Claimant(s)

Name(s) and Address(es) of Copyright Claimant(s): Give the name(s) and address(es) of the copyright claimant(s) in this work even if the claimant is the same as the author. Copyright in a work belongs initially to the author of the work (including, in the case of a work made for hire, the employer or other person for whom the work was prepared). The copyright claimant is either the author of the work or a person or organization to whom the copyright initially belonging to the author has been transferred.

Transfer: The statute provides that, if the copyright claimant is not the author, the application for registration must contain "a brief statement of how the claimant obtained ownership of the copyright." If any copyright claimant named in space 4 is not an author named in space 2, give a brief statement explaining how the claimant(s) obtained ownership of the copyright. Examples: "By written contract"; "Transfer of all rights by author"; "Assignment"; "By will." Do not attach transfer documents or other attachments or riders.

5 SPACE 5: Previous Registration

General Instructions: The questions in space 5 are intended to show whether an earlier registration has been made for this work and, if so, whether there is any basis for a new registration. As a general rule, only one basic copyright registration can be made for the same version of a particular work.

Same Version: If this version is substantially the same as the work covered by a previous registration, a second registration is not generally possible unless: (1) the work has been registered in unpublished form and a second registration is now being sought to cover this first published edition; or (2) someone other than the author is identified as copyright claimant in the earlier registration, and the author is now seeking registration in his or her own name. If either of these two exceptions applies, check the appropriate box and give the earlier registration number and date. Otherwise, do not submit Form PA; instead, write the Copyright Office

for information about supplementary registration or recordation of transfers of copyright ownership.

Changed Version: If the work has been changed and you are now seeking registration to cover the additions or revisions, check the last box in space 5, give the earlier registration number and date, and complete both parts of space 6 in accordance with the instructions below.

Previous Registration Number and Date: If more than one previous registration has been made for the work, give the number and date of the latest registration.

6 SPACE 6: Derivative Work or Compilation

General Instructions: Complete space 6 if this work is a "changed version," "compilation," or "derivative work," and if it incorporates one or more earlier works that have already been published or registered for copyright or that have fallen into the public domain. A "compilation" is defined as "a work formed by the collection and assembling of preexisting materials or of data that are selected, coordinated, or arranged in such a way that the resulting work as a whole constitutes an original work of authorship." A "derivative work" is "a work based on one or more preexisting works." Examples of derivative works include musical arrangements, dramatizations, translations, abridgments, condensations, motion picture versions, or "any other form in which a work may be recast, transformed, or adapted." Derivative works also include works "consisting of editorial revisions, annotations, or other modifications" if these changes, as a whole, represent an original work of authorship.

Preexisting Material (space 6a): Complete this space *and* space 6b for derivative works. In this space identify the preexisting work that has been recast, transformed, or adapted. For example, the preexisting material might be: "French version of Hugo's 'Le Roi s'amuse'." Do not complete this space for compilations.

Material Added to This Work (space 6b): Give a brief, general statement of the *additional* new material covered by the copyright claim for which registration is sought. In the case of a derivative work, identify this new material. Examples: "Arrangement for piano and orchestra"; "Dramatization for television"; "New film version"; "Revisions throughout; Act III completely new." If the work is a compilation, give a brief, general statement describing both the material that has been compiled *and* the compilation itself. Example: "Compilation of 19th Century Military Songs."

7, 8, 9 SPACE 7, 8, 9: Fee, Correspondence, Certification, Return Address

Deposit Account: If you maintain a Deposit Account in the Copyright Office, identify it in space 7a. Otherwise, leave the space blank and send the fee with your application and deposit.

Correspondence (space 7b): Give the name, address, area code, telephone number, fax number, and email address (if available) of the person to be consulted if correspondence about this application becomes necessary.

Certification (space 8): The application cannot be accepted unless it bears the date and the **handwritten signature** of the author or other copyright claimant, or of the owner of exclusive right(s), or of the duly authorized agent of the author, claimant, or owner of exclusive right(s).

Address for Return of Certificate (space 9): The address box must be completed legibly since the certificate will be returned in a window envelope.

MORE INFORMATION

How to Register a Recorded Work: If the musical or dramatic work that you are registering has been recorded (as a tape, disk, or cassette), you may choose either copyright application Form PA (Performing Arts) or Form SR (Sound Recordings), depending on the purpose of the registration.

Use Form PA to register the underlying musical composition or dramatic work. Form SR has been developed specifically to register a "sound recording" as defined by the Copyright Act—a work resulting from the "fixation of a series of sounds," separate and distinct from the underlying musical or dramatic work. Form SR should be used when the copyright claim is limited to the sound recording itself. (In one instance, Form SR may also be used to file for a copyright registration for both kinds of works—see (4) below.) Therefore:

(1) File Form PA if you are seeking to register the musical or dramatic work, not the "sound recording," even though what you deposit for copyright purposes may be in the form of a phonorecord.

(2) File Form PA if you are seeking to register the audio portion of an audiovisual work, such as a motion picture soundtrack; these are considered integral parts of the audiovisual work.

(3) File Form SR if you are seeking to register the "sound recording" itself, that is, the work that results from the fixation of a series of musical, spoken, or other sounds, but not the underlying musical or dramatic work.

(4) File Form SR if you are the copyright claimant for both the underlying musical or dramatic work and the sound recording, *and* you prefer to register both on the same form.

(5) File both forms PA and SR if the copyright claimant for the underlying work and sound recording differ, or you prefer to have separate registration for them.

"Copies" and "Phonorecords": To register for copyright, you are required to deposit "copies" or "phonorecords." These are defined as follows:

Musical compositions may be embodied (fixed) in "copies," objects from which a work can be read or visually perceived, directly or with the aid of a machine or device, such as manuscripts, books, sheet music, film, and videotape. They may also be fixed in "phonorecords," objects embodying fixations of sounds, such as tapes and phonograph disks, commonly known as phonograph records. For example, a song (the work to be registered) can be reproduced in sheet music ("copies") or phonograph records ("phonorecords"), or both.

Copyright Office fees are subject to change. For current fees, check the Copyright Office website at *www.copyright.gov*, write the Copyright Office, or call (202) 707-3000.

Ⓒ Form PA
For a Work of Performing Arts
UNITED STATES COPYRIGHT OFFICE

REGISTRATION NUMBER

PA   PAU

EFFECTIVE DATE OF REGISTRATION

Month   Day   Year

DO NOT WRITE ABOVE THIS LINE. IF YOU NEED MORE SPACE, USE A SEPARATE CONTINUATION SHEET.

1 TITLE OF THIS WORK ▼

PREVIOUS OR ALTERNATIVE TITLES ▼

NATURE OF THIS WORK ▼ See instructions

2 a NAME OF AUTHOR ▼

DATES OF BIRTH AND DEATH
Year Born ▼   Year Died ▼

Was this contribution to the work a "work made for hire"?
☐ Yes
☐ No

AUTHOR'S NATIONALITY OR DOMICILE
Name of Country
OR { Citizen of _____
Domiciled in _____

WAS THIS AUTHOR'S CONTRIBUTION TO THE WORK
Anonymous? ☐ Yes ☐ No
Pseudonymous? ☐ Yes ☐ No

If the answer to either of these questions is "Yes," see detailed instructions.

NATURE OF AUTHORSHIP Briefly describe nature of material created by this author in which copyright is claimed. ▼

NOTE

Under the law, the "author" of a "work made for hire" is generally the employer, not the employee (see instructions). For any part of this work that was "made for hire" check "Yes" in the space provided, give the employer (or other person for whom the work was prepared) as "Author" of that part, and leave the space for dates of birth and death blank.

b NAME OF AUTHOR ▼

DATES OF BIRTH AND DEATH
Year Born ▼   Year Died ▼

Was this contribution to the work a "work made for hire"?
☐ Yes
☐ No

AUTHOR'S NATIONALITY OR DOMICILE
Name of Country
OR { Citizen of _____
Domiciled in _____

WAS THIS AUTHOR'S CONTRIBUTION TO THE WORK
Anonymous? ☐ Yes ☐ No
Pseudonymous? ☐ Yes ☐ No

If the answer to either of these questions is "Yes," see detailed instructions.

NATURE OF AUTHORSHIP Briefly describe nature of material created by this author in which copyright is claimed. ▼

c NAME OF AUTHOR ▼

DATES OF BIRTH AND DEATH
Year Born ▼   Year Died ▼

Was this contribution to the work a "work made for hire"?
☐ Yes
☐ No

AUTHOR'S NATIONALITY OR DOMICILE
Name of Country
OR { Citizen of _____
Domiciled in _____

WAS THIS AUTHOR'S CONTRIBUTION TO THE WORK
Anonymous? ☐ Yes ☐ No
Pseudonymous? ☐ Yes ☐ No

If the answer to either of these questions is "Yes," see detailed instructions.

NATURE OF AUTHORSHIP Briefly describe nature of material created by this author in which copyright is claimed. ▼

3 a YEAR IN WHICH CREATION OF THIS WORK WAS COMPLETED This information must be given in all cases.
_____ Year

b DATE AND NATION OF FIRST PUBLICATION OF THIS PARTICULAR WORK
Complete this information ONLY if this work has been published.
Month _____ Day _____ Year _____
_____ Nation

4 COPYRIGHT CLAIMANT(S) Name and address must be given even if the claimant is the same as the author given in space 2. ▼

See instructions before completing this space.

TRANSFER If the claimant(s) named here in space 4 is (are) different from the author(s) named in space 2, give a brief statement of how the claimant(s) obtained ownership of the copyright. ▼

APPLICATION RECEIVED

ONE DEPOSIT RECEIVED

TWO DEPOSITS RECEIVED

FUNDS RECEIVED

DO NOT WRITE HERE
OFFICE USE ONLY

MORE ON BACK ▶ • Complete all applicable spaces (numbers 5-9) on the reverse side of this page.
• See detailed instructions. • Sign the form at line 8.

DO NOT WRITE HERE
Page 1 of _____ pages

Form PA

EXAMINED BY	FORM PA
CHECKED BY	
☐ CORRESPONDENCE Yes	FOR COPYRIGHT OFFICE USE ONLY

DO NOT WRITE ABOVE THIS LINE. IF YOU NEED MORE SPACE, USE A SEPARATE CONTINUATION SHEET.

5

PREVIOUS REGISTRATION Has registration for this work, or for an earlier version of this work, already been made in the Copyright Office?

☐ Yes ☐ No If your answer is "Yes," why is another registration being sought? (Check appropriate box.) ▼ If your answer is No, do **not** check box A, B, or C.

a. ☐ This is the first published edition of a work previously registered in unpublished form.

b. ☐ This is the first application submitted by this author as copyright claimant.

c. ☐ This is a changed version of the work, as shown by space 6 on this application.

If your answer is "Yes," give: **Previous Registration Number** ▼   **Year of Registration** ▼

6
a

DERIVATIVE WORK OR COMPILATION Complete both space 6a and 6b for a derivative work; complete only 6b for a compilation.
Preexisting Material Identify any preexisting work or works that this work is based on or incorporates. ▼

See instructions before completing this space.

b

Material Added to This Work Give a brief, general statement of the material that has been added to this work and in which copyright is claimed. ▼

7
a

DEPOSIT ACCOUNT If the registration fee is to be charged to a Deposit Account established in the Copyright Office, give name and number of Account.
Name ▼   **Account Number** ▼

b

CORRESPONDENCE Give name and address to which correspondence about this application should be sent. Name/Address/Apt/City/State/Zip▼

Area code and daytime telephone number   (   )   Fax number   (   )

Email

8

CERTIFICATION* I, the undersigned, hereby certify that I am the

Check only one ▶ {
☐ author
☐ other copyright claimant
☐ owner of exclusive right(s)
☐ authorized agent of _____
Name of author or other copyright claimant, or owner of exclusive right(s) ▲
}

of the work identified in this application and that the statements made by me in this application are correct to the best of my knowledge.

Typed or printed name and date ▼ If this application gives a date of publication in space 3, do not sign and submit it before that date.

_____ Date _____

Handwritten signature (X) ▼

x _____

9

Certificate will be mailed in window envelope to this address:

Name ▼

Number/Street/Apt ▼

City/State/Zip ▼

YOU MUST:
• Complete all necessary spaces
• Sign your application in space 8

SEND ALL 3 ELEMENTS IN THE SAME PACKAGE:
1. Application form
2. Nonrefundable filing fee in check or money order payable to *Register of Copyrights*
3. Deposit material

MAIL TO:
Library of Congress
Copyright Office
101 Independence Avenue SE
Washington, DC 20559-6000

Form PA – Full   Rev: 07/2006   Print: 07/2006 — xx,000   Printed on recycled paper

U.S. Government Printing Office: 2006-xxx-xxx/60,xxx

Instructions for Short Form PA

For works in the performing arts (except audiovisual works)

USE THIS FORM IF—

1. You are the *only* author and copyright owner of this work, *and*
2. The work was *not* made for hire, *and*
3. The work is completely new (does not contain a substantial amount of material that has been previously published or registered or is in the public domain) and is not an audiovisual work.

If any of the above does not apply, you must use standard Form PA.

NOTE: *Short Form PA is not appropriate for an anonymous author who does not wish to reveal his or her identity and may not be used for audiovisual works, including motion pictures.*

HOW TO COMPLETE SHORT FORM PA

• Type or print in black ink.
• Be clear and legible. (Your certificate of registration will be copied from your form.)
• Give only the information requested.

NOTE: You may use a continuation sheet (Form __/CON) to list individual titles in a collection. Complete Space A and list the individual titles under Space C on the back page. Space B is not applicable to short forms.

1 Title of This Work

You must give a title. If there is no title, state "UNTITLED." Alternative title: If the work is known by two titles, you also may give the second title. Or if the work has been published as part of a larger work, give the title of that larger work, in addition to the title of the contribution.

If you are registering an unpublished collection, give the collection title you want to appear in our records (for example: "Songs by Alice, Volume 1"). Be sure to keep a personal record of the songs you have included in the collection. If you want the certificate of registration to list the individual titles as well as the collection title, use a continuation sheet (Form___/CON).

2 Name and Address of Author and Owner of the Copyright

Give your name and mailing address. You may include your pseudonym followed by "pseud." Also, give the nation of which you are a citizen or where you have your domicile (i.e., permanent residence). Give daytime phone and fax numbers and email address, if available.

3 Year of Creation

Give the latest year in which you completed the work you are registering at this time. A work is "created" when it is written down, recorded, or otherwise "fixed" in a tangible form.

4 Publication

If the work has been published (i.e., if copies have been distributed to the public), give the complete date of publication (month, day, and year) and the nation where the publication first took place.

5 Type of Authorship in This Work

Check the box or boxes that describe the kind of material you are registering. Check *only* the authorship included in the copy, tape, or CD you are sending with the application. For example, if you are registering lyrics and plan to add music later, check only the box for "lyrics."

6 Signature of Author

Sign the application in black ink and check the appropriate box. The person signing the application should be the author or his/her authorized agent.

7 Person to Contact for Rights and Permissions

This space is optional. You may give the name and address of the person or organization to contact for permission to use the work. You may also provide phone, fax, or email information.

8 Certificate Will Be Mailed

This space must be completed. Your certificate of registration will be mailed in a window envelope to this address. Also, if the Copyright Office needs to contact you, we will write to this address.

9 Deposit Account

Complete this space only if you currently maintain a deposit account in the Copyright Office.

MAIL WITH THE FORM—

• The filing fee, in the form of a check or money order (*no cash*) payable to *Register of Copyrights,* and
• One or two copies of the work. If the work is unpublished, send one copy, tape, or CD. If published, send two copies of the best published edition if the work is in printed form, such as sheet music, or one copy of the best published edition if the work is recorded on a tape or disk.

Note: Inquire about special requirements for works first published outside the United States or before 1978. Copies submitted become the property of the U.S. Government.

Mail everything (application form, copy or copies, and fee) *in one package to: Library of Congress, Copyright Office, 101 Independence Avenue SE, Washington, DC 20559-6000*

QUESTIONS? Call (202) 707-3000 [TTY: (202) 707-6737] between 8:30 a.m. and 5:00 p.m. eastern time, Monday through Friday, except federal holidays. For forms and informational circulars, call (202) 707-9100 24 hours a day, 7 days a week, or download them at *www.copyright.gov.*

Form PA (Short Form)

Copyright Office fees are subject to change. For current fees, check the Copyright Office website at *www.copyright.gov*, write the Copyright Office, or call (202) 707-3000.

Short Form PA
For a Work of Performing Arts
UNITED STATES COPYRIGHT OFFICE

REGISTRATION NUMBER

PA   PAU

Effective Date of Registration

Application Received

Examined By

Deposit Received
One | Two

Correspondence ☐

Fee Received

TYPE OR PRINT IN BLACK INK. DO NOT WRITE ABOVE THIS LINE.

1   **Title of This Work:**

Alternative title or title of larger work in which this work was published:

2   **Name and Address of Author and Owner of the Copyright:**

Nationality or domicile:
Phone, fax, and email:

Phone ( )   Fax ( )

Email:

3   **Year of Creation:**

4   *If work has been published,* **Date and Nation of Publication:**

a. Date _____ _____ _____ *(Month, day, and year all required)*
                Month   Day   Year

b. Nation

5   **Type of Authorship in This Work:** Check all that this author created.

☐ Music   ☐ Other text (includes dramas, screenplays, etc.)
☐ Lyrics   *(If your work is a motion picture or other audiovisual work, use the Standard Form PA.)*

6   **Signature:** (Registration cannot be completed without a signature.)

I certify that the statements made by me in this application are correct to the best of my knowledge. * Check one:
☐ Author
☐ Authorized agent   **X** _ _ _ _ _ _ _ _ _ _ _ _ _ _ _ _ _ _ _

7   **Name and Address of Person to Contact for Rights and Permissions:**

Phone, fax, and email:

☐ Check here if same as #2 above.

Phone ( )   Fax ( )

Email:

OPTIONAL

8   Certificate will be mailed in window envelope to this address:

Name ▼

Number/Street/Apt ▼

City/State/Zip ▼

Complete this space only if you currently hold a Deposit Account in the Copyright Office.

9   Deposit Account # _____

Name _____

DO NOT WRITE HERE   Page 1 of _____ pages

*17 USC §506(e): Any person who knowingly makes a false representation of a material fact in the application for copyright registration provided for by section 409, or in any written statement filed in connection with the application, shall be fined not more than $2,500.

Form PA-Short   Rev: 07/2006   Print: 07/2006—••,000   Printed on recycled paper

U.S. Government Printing Office: 2006-•••••••/••,•••

Form SE

Detach and read these instructions before completing this form.
Make sure all applicable spaces have been filled in before you return this form.

BASIC INFORMATION

When to Use This Form: Use a separate Form SE for registration of each individual issue of a serial. A serial is defined as a work issued or intended to be issued in successive parts bearing numerical or chronological designations and intended to be continued indefinitely. This class includes a variety of works: periodicals; newspapers; annuals; the journals, proceedings, transactions, etc., of societies. Do not use Form SE to register an individual contribution to a serial. Request Form TX for such contributions.

Deposit to Accompany Application: An application for copyright registration must be accompanied by a deposit consisting of copies or phonorecords representing the entire work for which registration is to be made. The following are the general deposit requirements as set forth in the statute:

   Unpublished Work: Deposit one complete copy (or phonorecord).

   Published Work: Deposit two complete copies (or one phonorecord) of the best edition.

   Work First Published Outside the United States: Deposit one complete copy (or phonorecord) of the first foreign edition.

Mailing Requirements: It is important that you send the application, the deposit copy or copies, and the registration fee together in the same envelope or package. The Copyright Office cannot process them unless they are received together. Send to: *Library of Congress, Copyright Office, 101 Independence Avenue SE, Washington DC 20559-6000.*

The Copyright Notice: Before March 1, 1989, the use of copyright notice was mandatory on all published works, and any work first published before that date should have carried a notice. For works first published on and after March 1, 1989, use of the copyright notice is optional. For more information about copyright notice, see Circular 3, *Copyright Notices.*

For Further Information: To speak to an information specialist, call (202) 707-3000 (TTY: (202) 707-6737). Recorded information is available 24 hours a day. Order forms and other publications from the address in space 9 or call the Forms and Publications Hotline at (202) 707-2600 from a touchtone phone. Access and download circulars, forms, and other information from the Copyright Office website at *www.copyright.gov.*

LINE-BY-LINE INSTRUCTIONS

Please type or print using black ink. The form is used to produce the certificate.

1 SPACE 1: Title

Title of This Serial: Every work submitted for copyright registration must be given a title to identify that particular work. If the copies or phonorecords of the work bear a title (or an identifying phrase that could serve as a title), copy that wording *completely* and *exactly* on the application. Give the volume and number of the periodical issue for which you are seeking registration. The "Date on Copies" in space 1 should be the date appearing on the actual copies (for example: "June 1981," "Winter 1981"). Indexing of the registration and future identification of the work will depend on the information you give here.

Previous or Alternative Titles: Complete this space only if there are any additional titles for the serial under which someone searching for the registration might be likely to look or under which a document pertaining to the work might be recorded.

2 SPACE 2: Author(s)

General Instructions: After reading these instructions, decide who are the "authors" of this work for copyright purposes. In the case of a serial issue, the organization that directs the creation of the serial issue as a whole is generally considered the author of the "collective work" (see "Nature of Authorship") whether it employs a staff or uses the efforts of volunteers. Where, however, an individual is independently responsible for the serial issue, name that person as author of the "collective work."

Name of Author: The fullest form of the author's name should be given. In the case of a "work made for hire," the statute provides that "the employer or other person for whom the work was prepared is considered the author." If this issue is a "work made for hire," the author's name will be the full legal name of the hiring organization, corporation, or individual. The title of the periodical should not ordinarily be listed as "author" because the title itself does not usually correspond to a legal entity capable of authorship. When an individual creates an issue of a serial independently and not as an "employee" of an organization or corporation, that individual should be listed as the "author."

Author's Nationality or Domicile: Give the country of which the author is a citizen, or the country in which the author is domiciled. Nationality or domicile *must* be given in all cases. The citizenship of an organization formed under U.S. federal or state law should be stated as "U.S.A."

What is a "Work Made for Hire"? A "work made for hire" is defined as (1) "a work prepared by an employee within the scope of his or her employment"; or (2) "a work specially ordered or commissioned for use as a contribution to a collective work, as a part of a motion picture or other audiovisual work, as a translation, as a supplementary work, as a compilation, as an instructional text, as a test, as answer material for a test, or as an atlas, if the parties expressly agree in a written instrument signed by them that the work shall be considered a work made for hire." An organization that uses the efforts of volunteers in the creation of a "collective work" (see "Nature of Authorship") may also be considered the author of a "work made for hire" even though those volunteers were not specifically paid by the organization. In the case of a "work made for hire," give the full legal name of the employer and check "Yes" to indicate that the work was made for hire. You may also include the name of the employee along with the name of the employer (for example: "Elster Publishing Co., employer for hire of John Ferguson").

"Anonymous" or "Pseudonymous" Work: Leave this space *blank* if the serial is a "work made for hire." An author's contribution to a work is "anonymous" if that author is not identified on the copies or phonorecords of the work. An author's contribution to a work is "pseudonymous" if that author is identified on the copies or phonorecords under a fictitious name. If the work is "anonymous" you may: (1) leave the line blank; or (2) state "anonymous" on the line; or (3) reveal the author's identify. If the work is "pseudonymous" you may: (1) leave the line blank; or (2) give the pseudonym and identify it as such (for example: "Huntley Haverstock, pseudonym"); or (3) reveal the author's name, making clear which is the real name and which is the pseudonym (for example: "Judith Barton, whose pseudonym is Madeline Elster"). However, the citizenship or domicile of the author *must* be given in all cases.

Dates of Birth and Death: Leave this space blank if the author's contribution was a "work made for hire." If the author is dead, the statute requires that the year of death be included in the application unless the work is anonymous or pseudonymous. The author's birth date is optional but is useful as a form of identification.

Nature of Authorship: Give a brief statement of the nature of the particular author's contribution to the work. If an organization directed, controlled, and supervised the creation of the serial issue as a whole, check the box "collective work." The term "collective work" means that the author is responsible for compilation and editorial revision and may also be responsible for certain individual contributions to the serial issue. Further examples of "Authorship" which may apply both to organizational and to individual authors are "Entire text"; "Entire text and/or illustrations"; "Editorial revision, compilation, plus additional new material."

3 SPACE 3: Creation and Publication

General Instructions: Do not confuse "creation" with "publication." Every application for copyright registration must state "the year in which creation of the work was completed." Give the date and nation of first publication only if the work has been published.

Creation: Under the statute, a work is "created" when it is fixed in a copy or phonorecord for the first time. Where a work has been prepared over a period of time, the part of the work existing in fixed form on a particular date constitutes the created work on that date. The date you give here should be the year in which this particular issue was completed.

Publication: The statute defines "publication" as "the distribution of copies or phonorecords of a work to the public by sale or other transfer of ownership or by rental, lease, or lending"; a work is also "published" if there has been an "offering to distribute copies or phonorecords to a group of persons for purposes of further distribution, public performance, or public display." Give the full date (month, day, year) when, and the country where, publication of this particular issue first occurred. If first publication took place simultaneously in the United States and other countries, it is sufficient to state "U.S.A."

4 SPACE 4: Claimant(s)

Name(s) and Address(es) of Copyright Claimant(s): This space must be completed. Give the name(s) and address(es) of the copyright claimant(s) of this work even if the claimant is the same as the author named in space 2. Copyright in a work belongs initially to the author of the work (including, in the case of a work made for hire, the employer or other person for whom the work was prepared). The copyright claimant is either the author of the work or a person or organization to whom the copyright initially belonging to the author has been transferred.

Transfer: The statute provides that, if the copyright claimant is not the author, the application for registration must contain "a brief statement of how the claimant obtained ownership of the copyright." If any copyright claimant named in space 4 is not an author named in space 2, give a brief statement explaining how the claimant(s) obtained ownership of the copyright. Examples: "By written contract"; "Transfer of all rights by author"; "Assignment"; "By will." Do not attach transfer documents or other attachments or riders.

5 SPACE 5: Previous Registration

General Instructions: This space rarely applies to serials. Complete space 5 if this particular issue has been registered earlier or if it contains a substantial amount of material that has been previously registered. Do not complete this space if the previous registrations are simply those made for earlier issues.

Previous Registration:
a. Check this box if this issue has been registered in unpublished form and a second registration is now sought to cover the first published edition.

b. Check this box if someone other than the author is identified as copyright claimant in the earlier registration and the author is now seeking registration in his or her own name. If the work in question is a contribution to a collective work as opposed to the issue as a whole, file Form TX, not Form SE.

c. Check this box (and complete space 6) if this particular issue or a substantial portion of the material in it has been previously registered and you are now seeking registration for the additions and revisions which appear in this issue for the first time.

Previous Registration Number and Date: Complete this line if you checked one of the boxes above. If more than one previous registration has been made for the issue or for material in it, give only the number and year date for the latest registration.

6 SPACE 6: Derivative Work or Compilation

General Instructions: Complete space 6 if this issue is a "changed version," "compilation," or "derivative work" that incorporates one or more earlier works that have already been published or registered for copyright or that have fallen into the public domain. Do not complete space 6 for an issue consisting of entirely new material appearing for the first time such as a new issue of a continuing serial. A "compilation" is defined as "a work formed by the collection and assembling of preexisting materials or of data that are selected, coordinated, or arranged in such a way that the resulting work as a whole constitutes an original work of authorship." A "derivative work" is "a work based on one or more preexisting works." Examples of derivative works include translations, fictionalizations, abridgments, condensations, or "any other form in which a work may be recast, transformed, or adapted." Derivative works also include works "consisting of editorial revisions, annotations, or other modifications" if these changes, as a whole, represent an original work of authorship.

Preexisting Material (space 6a): For derivative works, complete this space *and* space 6b. In space 6a identify the preexisting work that has been recast, transformed, adapted, or updated. Example: "1978 Morgan Co. Sales Catalog." Do not complete space 6a for compilations.

Material Added to This Work (space 6b): Give a brief, general statement of the new material covered by the copyright claim for which registration is sought. *Derivative work* examples include: "Editorial revisions and additions to the Catalog"; "Translation"; "Additional material." If a periodical issue is a *compilation*, describe both the compilation itself and the material that has been compiled. Examples: "Compilation of previously published journal articles"; "Compilation of previously published data." An issue may be both a derivative work and a compilation, in which case a sample statement might be: "Compilation of [describe] and additional new material."

7, 8, 9 SPACE 7,8,9: Fee, Correspondence, Certification, Return Address

Deposit Account (Space 7a): If you maintain a deposit account in the Copyright Office, identify it in space 7a. Otherwise leave the space blank and send the fee with your application and deposit.

Correspondence (space 7b): This space should contain the name, address, area code, and telephone and fax number and email address of the person to be consulted if correspondence about this application becomes necessary.

Certification (space 8): The application cannot be accepted unless it bears the date and the *handwritten signature* of the author or other copyright claimant, or of the owner of exclusive right(s), or of the duly authorized agent of the author, claimant, or owner of exclusive right(s).

Address for Return of Certificate (space 9): The address box must be completed legibly since the certificate will be returned in a window envelope.

Form SE

Copyright Office fees are subject to change.
For current fees, check the Copyright Office
website at *www.copyright.gov*, write the Copyright Office, or call (202) 707-3000.

© Form SE
For a Serial
UNITED STATES COPYRIGHT OFFICE

REGISTRATION NUMBER

_____ U

EFFECTIVE DATE OF REGISTRATION

Month   Day   Year

DO NOT WRITE ABOVE THIS LINE. IF YOU NEED MORE SPACE, USE A SEPARATE CONTINUATION SHEET.

1   TITLE OF THIS SERIAL ▼

Volume ▼   Number ▼   Date of Copies ▼   Frequency of Publication ▼

PREVIOUS OR ALTERNATIVE TITLES ▼

---

2 a   NAME OF AUTHOR ▼   DATES OF BIRTH AND DEATH
Year Born ▼   Year Died ▼

Was this contribution to the work a   AUTHOR'S NATIONALITY OR DOMICILE   WAS THIS AUTHOR'S CONTRIBUTION TO
"work made for hire"?   Name of Country   THE WORK   If the answer to either
☐ Yes   OR { Citizen of ▶ _____   Anonymous?   ☐ Yes ☐ No   of these questions is
☐ No   { Domiciled in▶ _____   Pseudonymous? ☐ Yes ☐ No   "Yes," see detailed
                                                                                       instructions.

NATURE OF AUTHORSHIP Briefly describe nature of material created by this author in which copyright is claimed. ▼

NOTE

Under the law,
the "author" of
a "work made
for hire" is
generally the
employer, not
the employee
(see instruc-
tions). For any
part of this
work that was
"made for hire"
check "Yes" in
the space
provided, give
the employer
(or other
person for
whom the work
was prepared)
as "Author" of
that part, and
leave the
space for dates
of birth and
death blank.

b   NAME OF AUTHOR ▼   DATES OF BIRTH AND DEATH
Year Born ▼   Year Died ▼

Was this contribution to the work a   AUTHOR'S NATIONALITY OR DOMICILE   WAS THIS AUTHOR'S CONTRIBUTION TO
"work made for hire"?   Name of Country   THE WORK   If the answer to either
☐ Yes   OR { Citizen of ▶ _____   Anonymous?   ☐ Yes ☐ No   of these questions is
☐ No   { Domiciled in▶ _____   Pseudonymous? ☐ Yes ☐ No   "Yes," see detailed
                                                                                       instructions.

NATURE OF AUTHORSHIP Briefly describe nature of material created by this author in which copyright is claimed. ▼

c   NAME OF AUTHOR ▼   DATES OF BIRTH AND DEATH
Year Born ▼   Year Died ▼

Was this contribution to the work a   AUTHOR'S NATIONALITY OR DOMICILE   WAS THIS AUTHOR'S CONTRIBUTION TO
"work made for hire"?   Name of Country   THE WORK   If the answer to either
☐ Yes   OR { Citizen of ▶ _____   Anonymous?   ☐ Yes ☐ No   of these questions is
☐ No   { Domiciled in▶ _____   Pseudonymous? ☐ Yes ☐ No   "Yes," see detailed
                                                                                       instructions.

NATURE OF AUTHORSHIP Briefly describe nature of material created by this author in which copyright is claimed. ▼

---

3 a   YEAR IN WHICH CREATION OF THIS   DATE AND NATION OF FIRST PUBLICATION OF THIS PARTICULAR WORK
WORK WAS COMPLETED This information   **b** Complete this information   Month ▶ _____ Day▶ _____ Year▶ _____
                    must be given   ONLY if this work
_____ ◀Year in all cases.   has been published.   _____ ◀ Nation

4   COPYRIGHT CLAIMANT(S) Name and address must be given even if the claimant is the same as
the author given in space 2. ▼

See instructions
before completing
this space.

TRANSFER If the claimant(s) named here in space 4 is (are) different from the author(s) named in
space 2, give a brief statement of how the claimant(s) obtained ownership of the copyright. ▼

APPLICATION RECEIVED

ONE DEPOSIT RECEIVED

TWO DEPOSITS RECEIVED

FUNDS RECEIVED

DO NOT WRITE HERE
OFFICE USE ONLY

MORE ON BACK ▶ · Complete all applicable spaces (numbers 5–9) on the reverse side of this page.   DO NOT WRITE HERE
                · See detailed instructions.   · Sign the form at line 8.

Page 1 of _____ pages

Form SE

EXAMINED BY	FORM SE
CHECKED BY	
☐ CORRESPONDENCE Yes	FOR COPYRIGHT OFFICE USE ONLY

DO NOT WRITE ABOVE THIS LINE. IF YOU NEED MORE SPACE, USE A SEPARATE CONTINUATION SHEET.

PREVIOUS REGISTRATION Has registration for this work, or for an earlier version of this work, already been made in the Copyright Office?

☐ **Yes** ☐ **No** If your answer is "Yes," why is another registration being sought? (Check appropriate box.) ▼

a. ☐ This is the first published edition of a work previously registered in unpublished form.

b. ☐ This is the first application submitted by this author as copyright claimant.

c. ☐ This is a changed version of the work, as shown by space 6 on this application.

If your answer is "Yes," give: **Previous Registration Number** ▶   **Year of Registration** ▶

5

DERIVATIVE WORK OR COMPILATION Complete both space 6a and 6b for a derivative work; complete only 6b for a compilation.

Preexisting Material Identify any preexisting work or works that this work is based on or incorporates. ▼

a

6

Material Added to This Work Give a brief, general statement of the material that has been added to this work and in which copyright is claimed. ▼

b

See instructions
before completing
this space.

DEPOSIT ACCOUNT If the registration fee is to be charged to a Deposit Account established in the Copyright Office, give name and number of Account.

Name ▼   **Account Number** ▼

a

7

CORRESPONDENCE Give name and address to which correspondence about this application should be sent.   Name/Address/Apt/City/State/Zip ▼

b

Area code and daytime telephone number ▶   Fax number ▶

Email ▶

CERTIFICATION* I, the undersigned, hereby certify that I am the

Check only one ▶   { ☐ author
☐ other copyright claimant
☐ owner of exclusive right(s)
☐ authorized agent of _____

of the work identified in this application and that the statements made
by me in this application are correct to the best of my knowledge.

Name of author or other copyright claimant, or owner of exclusive right(s) ▲

8

Typed or printed name and date ▼ If this application gives a date of publication in space 3, do not sign and submit it before that date.

Date ▶ _____

Handwritten signature (X) ▼

X —

Certificate will be mailed in window envelope to this address:	Name ▼	**YOU MUST:** • Complete all necessary spaces • Sign your application in space 8	**9**
	Number/Street/Apt ▼	**SEND ALL 3 ELEMENTS IN THE SAME PACKAGE:** 1. Application form 2. Nonrefundable filing fee in check or money order payable to *Register of Copyrights* 3. Deposit material	
	City/State/Zip ▼	**MAIL TO:** Library of Congress Copyright Office 101 Independence Avenue SE Washington, DC 20559-6222	

*17 *USC* §506(e): Any person who knowingly makes a false representation of a material fact in the application for copyright registration provided for by section 409, or in any written statement filed in connection
with the application, shall be fined not more than $2,500.

Form SE–Full   Rev: 07/2006   Print: 07/2006   Printed on recycled paper   U.S. Government Printing Office: 2006-xxx-xxx/xx,xxx

Instructions for Short Form SE

Detach and read these instructions before completing this form.
Make sure all applicable spaces have been filled in before you return this form.

When to Use This Form: All the following conditions must be met in order to use this form. If any one of the conditions does not apply, you must use Form SE. Incorrect use of this form will result in a delay in your registration.

1. The claim must be in a collective work.

2. The work must be essentially an all-new collective work or issue.

3. The author must be a citizen or domiciliary of the United States.

4. The work must be a work made for hire.

5. The author(s) and claimant(s) must be the same person(s) or organization(s).

6. The work must be first published in the United States.

Deposit to Accompany Application: An application for registration of a copyright claim in a serial issue first published in the United States must be accompanied by a deposit consisting of two copies (or phonorecords) of the best edition.

Fee: The filing fee must be sent for each issue to be registered. Do not send cash or currency.

Mailing Requirements: Mail everything (application form, copy or copies, and fee) in one package to: *Library of Congress, Copyright Office, 101 Independence Avenue SE, Washington DC 20559-6000.*

Collective Work: The term "collective work" refers to a work, such as a serial issue, in which a number of contributions are assembled into a collective whole. A claim in the "collective work" extends to all copyrightable authorship created by employees of the author, as well as any independent contributions in which the claimant has acquired ownership of the copyright.

Publication: The statute defines "publication" as "the distribution of copies or phonorecords of a work to the public by sale or other transfer of ownership, or by rental, lease, or lending"; a work is also "published" if there has been an "offering to distribute copies or phonorecords to a group of persons for purposes of further distribution, public performance, or public display."

Creation: A work is "created" when it is fixed in a copy (or phonorecord) for the first time.

Work Made for Hire: A "work made for hire" is defined as: (1) a work prepared by an employee within the scope of his or her employment; or (2) a work specially ordered or commissioned for certain uses (including use as a contribution to a collective work), if the parties expressly agree in a written instrument signed by them that the work shall be considered a work made for hire. The employer is the author of a work made for hire.

The Copyright Notice: Before March 1, 1989, the use of copyright notice was mandatory on all published works, and any work first published before that date should have carried a notice. For works first published on and after March 1, 1989, use of the copyright notice is optional. For more information about copyright notice, see Circular 3, *Copyright Notices.*

For Further Information: To speak to an information specialist, call (202) 707-3000 (TTY: (202) 707-6737). Recorded information is available 24 hours a day. Order forms and other publications from the address at the bottom of page 2 or call the Forms and Publications Hotline at (202) 707-9100. Access and download circulars, forms, and other information from the Copyright Office website at *www.copyright.gov.*

SPACE-BY-SPACE INSTRUCTIONS

1 SPACE 1: Title

Every work submitted for copyright registration must be given a title to identify that particular work. Give the complete title of the periodical, including the volume, number, issue date, or other indicia printed on the copies. If possible, give the International Standard Serial Number (ISSN).

2 SPACE 2: Author and Copyright Claimant

Give the fullest form of the author and claimant's name. If there are joint authors and owners, give the names of all the author/owners. It is assumed that the authors and claimants are the same, that the work is made for hire, and that the claim is in the collective work.

3 SPACE 3: Date of Publication of This Particular Work

Give the exact date on which publication of this issue first took place. The full date, including month, day, and year must be given.

Year in Which Creation of This Issue Was Completed: Give the year in which this serial issue was first fixed in a copy or phonorecord. If no year is given, it is assumed that the issue was created in the same year in which it was published. The date must be the same as or no later than the publication date.

Certification: The application cannot be accepted unless it bears the handwritten signature of the copyright claimant or the duly authorized agent of the copyright claimant.

Person to Contact for Correspondence About This Claim: Give the name, daytime phone and fax numbers, and email address (if available) of the person to whom any correspondence concerning this claim should be addressed. Give the address only if it is different from the address for mailing of the certificate.

Deposit Account: Complete this space only if you currently maintain a deposit account in the Copyright Office. Otherwise, leave the space blank and forward the filing fee with your application and deposit.

Mailing Address of Certificate: This address must be complete and legible since the certificate will be mailed in a window envelope.

Form SE (Short Form)

Copyright Office fees are subject to change.
For current fees, check the Copyright Office
website at *www.copyright.gov*, write the Copyright Office, or call (202) 707-3000.

Ⓒ Short Form SE
For a Serial
UNITED STATES COPYRIGHT OFFICE

REGISTRATION NUMBER

_____

Effective Date of Registration

Examined By   Application Received

Correspondence ❑   Deposit Received
                           One | Two

                           Fee Received

DO NOT WRITE ABOVE THIS LINE.

1   **TITLE OF THIS SERIAL AS IT APPEARS ON THE COPY**

Volume▼   Number▼   Date on copies▼   ISSN▼

2   **NAME AND ADDRESS OF THE AUTHOR AND COPYRIGHT CLAIMANT IN THIS COLLECTIVE WORK MADE FOR HIRE**

3   **DATE OF PUBLICATION OF THIS PARTICULAR ISSUE**
Month ▼   Day ▼   Year ▼

YEAR IN WHICH CREATION OF
THIS ISSUE WAS COMPLETED (IF
EARLIER THAN THE YEAR OF
PUBLICATION):

Year ▶

CERTIFICATION*: I, the undersigned, hereby certify that I am the copyright claimant or the authorized agent of the copyright claimant of the work identified in this application, that all the conditions specified in the instructions on the back of this form are met, that the statements made by me in this application are correct to the best of my knowledge.

Handwritten signature (X) _____

Typed or printed name of signer _____

PERSON TO CONTACT FOR CORRESPONDENCE ABOUT THIS CLAIM
Name ▶ _____
Address (if other than given below) ▶ _____
Daytime phone ▶ (_____) _____
Fax ▶ (_____)   Email ▶ _____

DEPOSIT ACCOUNT
Account number ▶ _____
Name of account ▶ _____

Certificate
will be
mailed
in window
envelope
to this
address:

Name▼

Number/Street/Apt ▼

City/State/Zip▼

YOU MUST:
• Complete all necessary spaces
• Sign your application
**SEND ALL 3 ELEMENTS
IN THE SAME PACKAGE:**
1. Application form
2. Nonrefundable filing fee in check
or money order payable to *Register
of Copyrights*
3. Deposit material
MAIL TO:
Library of Congress
Copyright Office
101 Independence Avenue SE
Washington, DC 20559-6000

*17 *USC* §506(e): Any person who knowingly makes a false representation of a material fact in the application for copyright registration provided for by section 409, or in any written statement filed in connection with the application, shall be fined not more than $2,500.

Form SE-Short Rev: 07/2006 Print: 07/2006 — xx,000 Printed on recycled paper   U.S. Government Printing Office: 2006-xxx-xxx/xx,xxx

Form SR

Detach and read these instructions before completing this form.
Make sure all applicable spaces have been filled in before you return this form.

BASIC INFORMATION

When to Use This Form: Use Form SR for registration of published or unpublished sound recordings. It should be used when the copyright claim is limited to the sound recording itself, and it may also be used where the same copyright claimant is seeking simultaneous registration of the underlying musical, dramatic, or literary work embodied in the phonorecord.

With one exception, "sound recordings" are works that result from the fixation of a series of musical, spoken, or other sounds. The exception is for the audio portions of audiovisual works, such as a motion picture soundtrack or an audio cassette accompanying a filmstrip. These are considered a part of the audiovisual work as a whole.

Deposit to Accompany Application: An application for copyright registration must be accompanied by a deposit consisting of phonorecords representing the entire work for which registration is to be made.

Unpublished Work: Deposit one complete phonorecord.

Published Work: Deposit two complete phonorecords of the best edition, together with "any printed or other visually perceptible material" published with the phonorecords.

Work First Published Outside the United States: Deposit one complete phonorecord of the first foreign edition.

Contribution to a Collective Work: Deposit one complete phonorecord of the best edition of the collective work.

The Copyright Notice: Before March 1, 1989, the use of copyright notice was mandatory on all published works, and any work first published before that date should have carried a notice. For works first published on and after March 1, 1989, use of the copyright notice is optional. For more information about copyright notice, see Circular 3, *Copyright Notices.*

For Further Information: To speak to a Copyright Office staff member, call (202) 707-3000 (TTY: (202) 707-6737). Recorded information is available 24 hours a day. Order forms and other publications from Library of Congress, Copyright Office, 101 Independence Avenue SE, Washington, DC 20559-6000 or call the Forms and Publications Hotline at (202) 707-9100. Access and download circulars, forms, and other information from the Copyright Office website at *www.copyright.gov.*

PRIVACY ACT ADVISORY STATEMENT Required by the Privacy Act of 1974 (P.L. 93-579)
The authority for requesting this information is title 17 *USC*, secs. 409 and 410. Furnishing the requested information is voluntary. But if the information is not furnished, it may be necessary to delay or refuse registration and you may not be entitled to certain relief, remedies, and benefits provided in chapters 4 and 5 of title 17 *USC.*
The principal uses of the requested information are the establishment and maintenance of a public record and the examination of the application for compliance with the registration requirements of the copyright code.
Other routine uses include public inspection and copying, preparation of public indexes, preparation of public catalogs of copyright registrations, and preparation of search reports upon request.
NOTE: No other advisory statement will be given in connection with this application. Please keep this statement and refer to it if we communicate with you regarding this application.

LINE-BY-LINE INSTRUCTIONS

Please type or print neatly using black ink. The form is used to produce the certificate.

1 SPACE 1: Title

Title of This Work: Every work submitted for copyright registration must be given a title to identify that particular work. If the phonorecords or any accompanying printed material bears a title (or an identifying phrase that could serve as a title), transcribe that wording completely and exactly on the application. Indexing of the registration and future identification of the work may depend on the information you give here.

Previous, Alternative, or Contents Titles: Complete this space if there are any previous or alternative titles for the work under which someone searching for the registration might be likely to look, or under which a work pertaining to the work might be recorded. You may also give the individual contents titles, if any, in this space or you may use a Continuation Sheet. Circle the term that describes the titles given.

2 SPACE 2: Author(s)

General Instructions: After reading these instructions, decide who are the "authors" of this work for copyright purposes. Then, unless the work is a "collective work," give the requested information about every "author" who contributed any appreciable amount of copyrightable matter to this version of the work. If you need further space, request additional Continuation Sheets. In the case of a collective work such as a collection of previously published or registered sound recordings, give information about the author of the collective work as a whole. If you are submitting this Form SR to cover the recorded musical, dramatic, or literary work as well as the sound recording itself, it is important for space 2 to include full information about the various authors of all of the material covered by the copyright claim, making clear the nature of each author's contribution.

Name of Author: The fullest form of the author's name should be given. Unless the work was "made for hire," the individual who actually created the work is its "author." In the case of a work made for hire, the statute provides that "the employer or other person for whom the work was prepared is considered the author."

What Is a "Work Made for Hire"? A "work made for hire" is defined as: (1) "a work prepared by an employee within the scope of his or her employment"; or (2) "a work specially ordered or commissioned for use as a contribution to a collective work, as a part of a motion picture or other audiovisual work, as a translation, as a supplementary work, as a compilation, as an instructional text, as a test, as answer material for a test, or as an atlas, if the parties expressly agree in a written instrument signed by them that the work shall be considered a work made for hire." If you have checked "Yes" to indicate that the work was "made for hire," you must give the full legal name of the employer (or other person for whom the work was prepared). You may also include the name of the employee along with the name of the employer (for example: "Elster Record Co., employer for hire of John Ferguson").

"Anonymous" or "Pseudonymous" Work: An author's contribution to a work is "anonymous" if that author is not identified on the copies or phonorecords of the work. An author's contribution to a work is "pseudonymous" if that author is identified on the copies or phonorecords under a fictitious name. If the work is "anonymous" you may: (1) leave the line blank; or (2) state "anonymous" on the line; or (3) reveal the author's identity. If the work is "pseudonymous" you may: (1) leave the line blank; or (2) give the pseudonym and identify it as such (for example: "Huntley Haverstock, pseudonym"); or (3) reveal the author's name, making clear which is the real name and which is the pseudonym (for example: "Judith Barton, whose pseudonym is Madeline Elster"). However, the citizenship or domicile of the author *must* be given in all cases.

Dates of Birth and Death: If the author is dead, the statute requires that the year of death be included in the application unless the work is anonymous or pseudonymous. The author's birth date is optional, but is useful as a form of identification. Leave this space blank if the author's contribution was a "work made for hire."

Author's Nationality or Domicile: Give the country in which the author is a citizen, or the country in which the author is domiciled. Nationality or domicile *must* be given in all cases.

Nature of Authorship: Sound recording authorship is the performance, sound production, or both, that is fixed in the recording deposited for registration. Describe this authorship in space 2 as "sound recording." If the claim also covers the underlying work(s), include the appropriate authorship terms for each author, for example, "words," "music," "arrangement of music," or "text."

Generally, for the claim to cover both the sound recording and the underlying work(s), every author should have contributed to both the sound recording *and* the underlying work(s). If the claim includes artwork or photographs, include the appropriate term in the statement of authorship.

3 SPACE 3: Creation and Publication

General Instructions: Do not confuse "creation" with "publication." Every application for copyright registration must state "the year in which creation of the work was completed." Give the date and nation of first publication only if the work has been published.

Creation: Under the statute, a work is "created" when it is fixed in a copy or phonorecord for the first time. Where a work has been prepared over a period of time, the part of the work existing in fixed form on a particular date constitutes the created work on that date. The date you give here should be the year in which the author completed the particular version for which registration is now being sought, even if other versions exist or if further changes or additions are planned.

Publication: The statute defines "publication" as "the distribution of copies or phonorecords of a work to the public by sale or other transfer of ownership, or by rental, lease, or lending"; a work is also "published" if there has been an "offering to distribute copies or phonorecords to a group of persons for purposes of further distribution, public performance, or public display." Give the full date (month, date, year) when, and the country where, publication first occurred. If first publication took place simultaneously in the United States and other countries, it is sufficient to state "U.S.A."

4 SPACE 4: Claimant(s)

Name(s) and Address(es) of Copyright Claimant(s): Give the name(s) and address(es) of the copyright claimant(s) in the work even if the claimant is the same as the author. Copyright in a work belongs initially to the author of the work (including, in the case of a work made for hire, the employer or other person for whom the work was prepared). The copyright claimant is either the author of the work or a person or organization to whom the copyright initially belonging to the author has been transferred.

Transfer: The statute provides that, if the copyright claimant is not the author, the application for registration must contain "a brief statement of how the claimant obtained ownership of the copyright." If any copyright claimant named in space 4a is not an author named in space 2, give a brief statement explaining how the claimant(s) obtained ownership of the copyright. Examples: "By written contract"; "Transfer of all rights by author"; "Assignment"; "By will." Do not attach transfer documents or other attachments or riders.

5 SPACE 5: Previous Registration

General Instructions: The questions in space 5 are intended to show whether an earlier registration has been made for this work and, if so, whether there is any basis for a new registration. As a rule, only one basic copyright registration can be made for the same version of a particular work.

Same Version: If this version is substantially the same as the work covered by a previous registration, a second registration is not generally possible unless: (1) the work has been registered in unpublished form and a second registration is now being sought to cover this first published edition; or (2) someone other than the author is identified as copyright claimant in the earlier registration and the author is now seeking registration in his or her own name. If either of these two exceptions applies, check the appropriate box and give the earlier registration number and date. Otherwise, do not submit Form SR. Instead, write the Copyright Office for information about supplementary registration or recordation of transfers of copyright ownership.

Changed Version: If the work has been changed and you are now seeking reg-

istration to cover the additions or revisions, check the last box in space 5, give the earlier registration number and date, and complete both parts of space 6 in accordance with the instructions below.

Previous Registration Number and Date: If more than one previous registration has been made for the work, give the number and date of the latest registration.

6 SPACE 6: Derivative Work or Compilation

General Instructions: Complete space 6 if this work is a "changed version," "compilation," or "derivative work," and if it incorporates one or more earlier works that have already been published or registered for copyright, or that have fallen into the public domain, or sound recordings that were fixed before February 15, 1972. A "compilation" is defined as "a work formed by the collection and assembling of preexisting materials or of data that are selected, coordinated, or arranged in such a way that the resulting work as a whole constitutes an original work of authorship." A "derivative work" is "a work based on one or more preexisting works." Examples of derivative works include recordings reissued with substantial editorial revisions or abridgments of the recorded sounds, and recordings republished with new recorded material, or "any other form in which a work may be recast, transformed, or adapted." Derivative works also include works "consisting of editorial revisions, annotations, or other modifications" if these changes, as a whole, represent an original work of authorship.

Preexisting Material (space 6a): Complete this space *and* space 6b for derivative works. In this space identify the preexisting work that has been recast, transformed, or adapted. The preexisting work may be material that has been previously published, previously registered, or that is in the public domain. For example, the preexisting material might be: "1970 recording by Sperryville Symphony of Bach Double Concerto."

Material Added to This Work (space 6b): Give a brief, general statement of the **additional** new material covered by the copyright claim for which registration is sought. In the case of a derivative work, identify this new material. Examples: "Recorded performances on bands 1 and 3"; "Remixed sounds from original multitrack sound sources"; "New words, arrangement, and additional sounds." If the work is a compilation, give a brief, general statement describing both the material that has been compiled *and* the compilation itself. Example: "Compilation of 1938 Recordings by various swing bands."

7, 8, 9 SPACE 7, 8, 9: Fee, Correspondence, Certification, Return Address

Deposit Account: If you maintain a Deposit Account in the Copyright Office, identify it in space 7a. Otherwise, leave the space blank and send the filing fee with your application and deposit. (See space 8 on form.) (**Note:** Copyright Office fees are subject to change. For current fees, check the Copyright Office website at *www.copyright.gov*, write the Copyright Office, or call (202) 707-3000.)

Correspondence (space 7b): Give the name, address, area code, telephone number, fax number, and email address (if available) of the person to be consulted if correspondence about this application becomes necessary.

Certification (space 8): This application cannot be accepted unless it bears the date and the *handwritten signature* of the author or other copyright claimant, or of the owner of exclusive right(s), or of the duly authorized agent of the author, claimant, or owner of exclusive right(s).

Address for Return of Certificate (space 9): The address box must be completed legibly since the certificate will be returned in a window envelope.

MORE INFORMATION

"Works": "Works" are the basic subject matter of copyright; they are what authors create and copyright protects. The statute draws a sharp distinction between the "work" and "any material object in which the work is embodied."

"Copies" and "Phonorecords": These are the two types of material objects in which "works" are embodied. In general, "copies" are objects from which a work can be read or visually perceived, directly or with the aid of a machine or device, such as manuscripts, books, sheet music, film, and videotape. "Phonorecords" are objects embodying fixations of sounds, such as audio tapes and phonograph disks. For example, a song (the "work") can be reproduced in sheet music ("copies") or phonograph disks ("phonorecords"), or both.

"Sound Recordings": These are "works," not "copies" or "phonorecords." "Sound recordings" are "works that result from the fixation of a series of musical, spoken, or other sounds, but not including the sounds accompanying a motion picture or other audiovisual work." Example: When a record company issues a new release, the release will typically involve two distinct "works": the "musical work" that has been recorded, and the "sound recording" as a separate work in itself. The material objects that the record company sends out are "phonorecords": physical reproductions of both the "musical work" and the "sound recording."

Should You File More Than One Application? If your work consists of a recorded musical, dramatic, or literary work and if both that "work" and the sound recording as a separate "work" are eligible for registration, the application form you should file depends on the following:

File Only Form SR if: The copyright claimant is the same for both the musical, dramatic, or literary work and for the sound recording, and you are seeking a single registration to cover both of these "works."

File Only Form PA (or Form TX) if: You are seeking to register only the musical, dramatic, or literary work, not the sound recording. Form PA is appropriate for works of the performing arts; Form TX is for nondramatic literary works.

Separate Applications Should Be Filed on Form PA (or Form TX) and on Form SR if: (1) The copyright claimant for the musical, dramatic, or literary work is different from the copyright claimant for the sound recording; or (2) You prefer to have separate registrations for the musical, dramatic, or literary work and for the sound recording.

Form SR

Copyright Office fees are subject to change. For current fees, check the Copyright Office website at *www.copyright.gov*, write the Copyright Office, or call (202) 707-3000.

Form SR
For a Sound Recording
UNITED STATES COPYRIGHT OFFICE

REGISTRATION NUMBER

_____

SR   SRU

EFFECTIVE DATE OF REGISTRATION

_____

Month   Day   Year

DO NOT WRITE ABOVE THIS LINE. IF YOU NEED MORE SPACE, USE A SEPARATE CONTINUATION SHEET.

1

TITLE OF THIS WORK ▼

_____

PREVIOUS, ALTERNATIVE, OR CONTENTS TITLES (CIRCLE ONE) ▼

2   a

NAME OF AUTHOR ▼

DATES OF BIRTH AND DEATH
Year Born ▼   Year Died ▼

Was this contribution to the work a "work made for hire"?
☐ Yes
☐ No

AUTHOR'S NATIONALITY OR DOMICILE
Name of Country
OR ⎰ Citizen of ▶ _____
   ⎱ Domiciled in ▶ _____

WAS THIS AUTHOR'S CONTRIBUTION TO THE WORK
Anonymous?   ☐ Yes ☐ No
Pseudonymous?   ☐ Yes ☐ No
If the answer to either of these questions is "Yes," see detailed instructions.

NATURE OF AUTHORSHIP   Briefly describe nature of material created by this author in which copyright is claimed. ▼

NOTE

Under the law, the "author" of a "work made for hire" is generally the employer, not the employee (see instructions). For any part of this work that was "made for hire," check "Yes" in the space provided, give the employer (or other person for whom the work was prepared) as "Author" of that part, and leave the space for dates of birth and death blank.

b

NAME OF AUTHOR ▼

DATES OF BIRTH AND DEATH
Year Born ▼   Year Died ▼

Was this contribution to the work a "work made for hire"?
☐ Yes
☐ No

AUTHOR'S NATIONALITY OR DOMICILE
Name of Country
OR ⎰ Citizen of ▶ _____
   ⎱ Domiciled in ▶ _____

WAS THIS AUTHOR'S CONTRIBUTION TO THE WORK
Anonymous?   ☐ Yes ☐ No
Pseudonymous?   ☐ Yes ☐ No
If the answer to either of these questions is "Yes," see detailed instructions.

NATURE OF AUTHORSHIP   Briefly describe nature of material created by this author in which copyright is claimed. ▼

c

NAME OF AUTHOR ▼

DATES OF BIRTH AND DEATH
Year Born ▼   Year Died ▼

Was this contribution to the work a "work made for hire"?
☐ Yes
☐ No

AUTHOR'S NATIONALITY OR DOMICILE
Name of Country
OR ⎰ Citizen of ▶ _____
   ⎱ Domiciled in ▶ _____

WAS THIS AUTHOR'S CONTRIBUTION TO THE WORK
Anonymous?   ☐ Yes ☐ No
Pseudonymous?   ☐ Yes ☐ No
If the answer to either of these questions is "Yes," see detailed instructions.

NATURE OF AUTHORSHIP   Briefly describe nature of material created by this author in which copyright is claimed. ▼

3   a

YEAR IN WHICH CREATION OF THIS WORK WAS COMPLETED
_____ ◀ Year
This information must be given in all cases.

b
DATE AND NATION OF FIRST PUBLICATION OF THIS PARTICULAR WORK
Complete this information ONLY if this work has been published.
Month ▶ _____ Day ▶ _____ Year ▶ _____ ◀ Nation

4   a

See instructions before completing this space.

COPYRIGHT CLAIMANT(S) Name and address must be given even if the claimant is the same as the author given in space 2. ▼

b

TRANSFER If the claimant(s) named here in space 4 is (are) different from the author(s) named in space 2, give a brief statement of how the claimant(s) obtained ownership of the copyright. ▼

APPLICATION RECEIVED

ONE DEPOSIT RECEIVED

TWO DEPOSITS RECEIVED

FUNDS RECEIVED

DO NOT WRITE HERE OFFICE USE ONLY

MORE ON BACK ▶   · Complete all applicable spaces (numbers 5-9) on the reverse side of this page.
· See detailed instructions.   · Sign the form at line 8.

DO NOT WRITE HERE
Page 1 of _____ pages

Form SR

EXAMINED BY	FORM SR
CHECKED BY	
CORRESPONDENCE ❑ Yes	FOR COPYRIGHT OFFICE USE ONLY

DO NOT WRITE ABOVE THIS LINE. IF YOU NEED MORE SPACE, USE A SEPARATE CONTINUATION SHEET.

PREVIOUS REGISTRATION Has registration for this work, or for an earlier version of this work, already been made in the Copyright Office?

❑ Yes ❑ No If your answer is "Yes," why is another registration being sought? (Check appropriate box) ▼

a. ❑ This work was previously registered in unpublished form and now has been published for the first time.

b. ❑ This is the first application submitted by this author as copyright claimant.

c. ❑ This is a changed version of the work, as shown by space 6 on this application.

If your answer is "Yes," give: **Previous Registration Number** ▼   **Year of Registration** ▼

5

DERIVATIVE WORK OR COMPILATION
Preexisting Material Identify any preexisting work or works that this work is based on or incorporates. ▼

a

Material Added to This Work Give a brief, general statement of the material that has been added to this work and in which copyright is claimed. ▼

b

6

See instructions
before completing
this space.

DEPOSIT ACCOUNT If the registration fee is to be charged to a deposit account established in the Copyright Office, give name and number of Account.
          Name ▼   **Account Number** ▼

a

CORRESPONDENCE Give name and address to which correspondence about this application should be sent.   Name/Address/Apt/City/State/Zip ▼

b

          Area code and daytime telephone number   Fax number
          Email

7

CERTIFICATION* I, the undersigned, hereby certify that I am the

Check only one ▼

❑ author   ❑ owner of exclusive right(s)

❑ other copyright claimant   ❑ authorized agent of _____
                              Name of author or other copyright claimant, or owner of exclusive right(s) ▲

of the work identified in this application and that the statements made by me in this application are correct to the best of my knowledge.

Typed or printed name and date ▼ If this application gives a date of publication in space 3, do not sign and submit it before that date.

_____   Date _____

          Handwritten signature (x) ▼

X _

8

Certificate will be mailed in window envelope to this address	Name ▼	YOU MUST: • Complete all necessary spaces • Sign your application in space 8
	Number/Street/Apt ▼	SEND ALL 3 ELEMENTS IN THE SAME PACKAGE: 1. Application form 2. Nonrefundable filing fee in check or money order payable to *Register of Copyrights* 3. Deposit material
	City/State/Zip ▼	MAIL TO: Library of Congress Copyright Office 101 Independence Avenue SE Washington, DC 20559-6000

9

*17 *USC* §506(e): Any person who knowingly makes a false representation of a material fact in the application for copyright registration provided for by section 409, or in any written statement filed in connection with the application, shall be fined not more than $2,500.

Form SR-Full   Rev: 07/2006   Print: 07/2006—xx,000   Printed on recycled paper   U.S. Government Printing Office: 2005-xxx-xxx/60,xxx

Form VA

Detach and read these instructions before completing this form.
Make sure all applicable spaces have been filled in before you return this form.

BASIC INFORMATION

When to Use This Form: Use Form VA for copyright registration of published or unpublished works of the visual arts. This category consists of "pictorial, graphic, or sculptural works," including two-dimensional and three-dimensional works of fine, graphic, and applied art, photographs, prints and art reproductions, maps, globes, charts, technical drawings, diagrams, and models.

What Does Copyright Protect? Copyright in a work of the visual arts protects those pictorial, graphic, or sculptural elements that, either alone or in combination, represent an "original work of authorship." The statute declares: "In no case does copyright protection for an original work of authorship extend to any idea, procedure, process, system, method of operation, concept, principle, or discovery, regardless of the form in which it is described, explained, illustrated, or embodied in such work."

Works of Artistic Craftsmanship and Designs: "Works of artistic craftsmanship" are registrable on Form VA, but the statute makes clear that protection extends to "their form" and not to "their mechanical or utilitarian aspects." The "design of a useful article" is considered copyrightable "only if, and only to the extent that, such design incorporates pictorial, graphic, or sculptural features that can be identified separately from, and are capable of existing independently of, the utilitarian aspects of the article."

Labels and Advertisements: Works prepared for use in connection with the sale or advertisement of goods and services are registrable if they contain "original work of authorship." Use Form VA if the copyrightable material in the work you are registering is mainly pictorial or graphic; use Form TX if it consists mainly of text. **Note:** Words and short phrases such as names, titles, and slogans cannot be protected by copyright, and the same is true of standard symbols, emblems, and other commonly used graphic designs that are in the public domain. When used commercially, material of that sort can sometimes be protected under state laws of unfair competition or under the federal trademark laws. For information about trademark registration, write to the U.S. Patent and Trademark Office, PO Box 1450, Alexandria, VA 22313-1450.

Architectural Works: Copyright protection extends to the design of buildings created for the use of human beings. Architectural works created on or after December 1, 1990, or that on December 1, 1990, were unconstructed and embodied only in unpublished plans or drawings are eligible. Request Circular 41, *Copyright Claims in Architectural Works*, for more information. Architectural works and technical drawings cannot be registered on the same application.

Deposit to Accompany Application: An application for copyright registration must be accompanied by a deposit consisting of copies representing the entire work for which registration is to be made.

   Unpublished Work: Deposit one complete copy.

   Published Work: Deposit two complete copies of the best edition.

   Work First Published Outside the United States: Deposit one complete copy of the first foreign edition.

   Contribution to a Collective Work: Deposit one complete copy of the best edition of the collective work.

The Copyright Notice: Before March 1, 1989, the use of copyright notice was mandatory on all published works, and any work first published before that date should have carried a notice. For works first published on and after March 1, 1989, use of the copyright notice is optional. For more information about copyright notice, see Circular 3, *Copyright Notice*.

For Further Information: To speak to a Copyright Office staff member, call (202) 707-3000 (TTY: (202) 707-6737). Recorded information is available 24 hours a day. Order forms and other publications from the address in space 9 or call the Forms and Publications Hotline at (202) 707-9100. Access and download circulars, forms, and other information from the Copyright Office website at *www.copyright.gov*.

LINE-BY-LINE INSTRUCTIONS

Please type or print using black ink. The form is used to produce the certificate.

1 SPACE 1: Title

Title of This Work: Every work submitted for copyright registration must be given a title to identify that particular work. If the copies of the work bear a title (or an identifying phrase that could serve as a title), transcribe that wording *completely* and *exactly* on the application. Indexing of the registration and future identification of the work will depend on the information you give here. For an architectural work that has been constructed, add the date of construction after the title; if unconstructed at this time, add "not yet constructed."

Publication as a Contribution: If the work being registered is a contribution to a periodical, serial, or collection, give the title of the contribution in the "Title of This Work" space. Then, in the line headed "Publication as a Contribution," give information about the collective work in which the contribution appeared.

Nature of This Work: Briefly describe the general nature or character of the pictorial, graphic, or sculptural work being registered for copyright. Examples: "Oil Painting"; "Charcoal Drawing"; "Etching"; "Sculpture"; "Map"; "Photograph"; "Scale Model"; "Lithographic Print"; "Jewelry Design"; "Fabric Design."

Previous or Alternative Titles: Complete this space if there are any additional titles for the work under which someone searching for the registration might be likely to look, or under which a document pertaining to the work might be recorded.

2 SPACE 2: Author(s)

General Instruction: After reading these instructions, decide who are the "authors" of this work for copyright purposes. Then, unless the work is a "collective work," give the requested information about every "author" who contributed any appreciable amount of copyrightable matter to this version of the work. If you need further space, request Continuation Sheets. In the case of a collective work, such as a catalog of paintings or collection of cartoons by various authors, give information about the author of the collective work as a whole.

Name of Author: The fullest form of the author's name should be given. Unless the work was "made for hire," the individual who actually created the work is its "author." In the case of a work made for hire, the statute provides that "the employer or other person for whom the work was prepared is considered the author."

What Is a "Work Made for Hire"? A "work made for hire" is defined as: (1) "a work prepared by an employee within the scope of his or her employment"; or (2) "a work specially ordered or commissioned for use as a contribution to a collective work, as a part of a motion picture or other audiovisual work, as a translation, as a supplementary work, as a compilation, as an instructional text, as a test, as answer material for a test, or as an atlas, if the parties expressly agree in a written instrument signed by them that the work shall be considered a work made for hire." If you have checked "Yes" to indicate that the work was "made for hire," you must give the full legal name of the employer (or other person for whom the work was prepared). You may also include the name of the employee along with the name of the employer (for example: "Elster Publishing Co., employer for hire of John Ferguson").

"Anonymous" or "Pseudonymous" Work: An author's contribution to a work is "anonymous" if that author is not identified on the copies or phonorecords of the work. An author's contribution to a work is "pseudonymous" if that author is identified on the copies or phonorecords under a fictitious name. If the work is "anonymous" you may: (1) leave the line blank; or (2) state "anonymous" on the line; or (3) reveal the author's identity. If the work is "pseudonymous" you may: (1) leave the line blank; or (2) give the pseudonym and identify it as such (for example: "Huntley Haverstock, pseudonym"); or (3) reveal the author's name, making clear which is the real name and which is the pseudonym (for example: "Henry Leek, whose pseudonym is Priam Farrel"). However, the citizenship or domicile of the author *must* be given in all cases.

Dates of Birth and Death: If the author is dead, the statute requires that the year of death be included in the application unless the work is anonymous or pseudonymous. The author's birth date is optional but is useful as a form of identification. Leave this space blank if the author's contribution was a "work made for hire."

Form VA

Author's Nationality or Domicile: Give the country of which the author is a citizen or the country in which the author is domiciled. Nationality or domicile *must* be given in all cases.

Nature of Authorship: Categories of pictorial, graphic, and sculptural authorship are listed below. Check the box(es) that best describe(s) each author's contribution to the work.

3-Dimensional sculptures: fine art sculptures, toys, dolls, scale models, and sculptural designs applied to useful articles.

2-Dimensional artwork: watercolor and oil paintings; pen and ink drawings; logo illustrations; greeting cards; collages; stencils; patterns; computer graphics; graphics appearing in screen displays; artwork appearing on posters, calendars, games, commercial prints and labels, and packaging, as well as 2-dimensional artwork applied to useful articles, and designs reproduced on textiles, lace, and other fabrics; on wallpaper, carpeting, floor tile, wrapping paper, and clothing.

Reproductions of works of art: reproductions of preexisting artwork made by, for example, lithography, photoengraving, or etching.

Maps: cartographic representations of an area, such as state and county maps, atlases, marine charts, relief maps, and globes.

Photographs: pictorial photographic prints and slides and holograms.

Jewelry designs: 3-dimensional designs applied to rings, pendants, earrings, necklaces, and the like.

Technical drawings: diagrams illustrating scientific or technical information in linear form, such as architectural blueprints or mechanical drawings.

Text: textual material that accompanies pictorial, graphic, or sculptural works, such as comic strips, greeting cards, games rules, commercial prints or labels, and maps.

Architectural works: designs of buildings, including the overall form as well as the arrangement and composition of spaces and elements of the design.

NOTE: Any registration for the underlying architectural plans must be applied for on a separate Form VA, checking the box "Technical drawing."

SPACE 3: Creation and Publication

General Instructions: Do not confuse "creation" with "publication." Every application for copyright registration must state "the year in which creation of the work was completed." Give the date and nation of first publication only if the work has been published.

Creation: Under the statute, a work is "created" when it is fixed in a copy or phonorecord for the first time. Where a work has been prepared over a period of time, the part of the work existing in fixed form on a particular date constitutes the created work on that date. The date you give here should be the year in which the author completed the particular version for which registration is now being sought, even if other versions exist or if further changes or additions are planned.

Publication: The statute defines "publication" as "the distribution of copies or phonorecords of a work to the public by sale or other transfer of ownership, or by rental, lease, or lending"; a work is also "published" if there has been an "offering to distribute copies or phonorecords to a group of persons for purposes of further distribution, public performance, or public display." Give the full date (month, day, year) when, and the country where, publication first occurred. If first publication took place simultaneously in the United States and other countries, it is sufficient to state "U.S.A."

SPACE 4: Claimant(s)

Name(s) and Address(es) of Copyright Claimant(s): Give the name(s) and address(es) of the copyright claimant(s) in this work even if the claimant is the same as the author. Copyright in a work belongs initially to the author of the work (including, in the case of a work made for hire, the employer or other person for whom the work was prepared). The copyright claimant is either the author of the work or a person or organization to whom the copyright initially belonging to the author has been transferred.

Transfer: The statute provides that, if the copyright claimant is not the author, the application for registration must contain "a brief statement of how the claimant obtained ownership of the copyright." If any copyright claimant named in space 4 is not an author named in space 2, give a brief statement explaining how the claimant(s) obtained ownership of the copyright. Examples: "By written contract"; "Transfer of all rights by author"; "Assignment"; "By will." Do not attach transfer documents or other attachments or riders.

SPACE 5: Previous Registration

General Instructions: The questions in space 5 are intended to find out whether an earlier registration has been made for this work and, if so, whether there is any basis for a new registration. As a rule, only one basic copyright registration can be made for the same version of a particular work.

Same Version: If this version is substantially the same as the work covered by a previous registration, a second registration is not generally possible unless: (1) the work has been registered in unpublished form and a second registration is now being sought to cover this first published edition; or (2) someone other than the author is identified as a copyright claimant in the earlier registration, and the author is now seeking registration in his or her own name. If either of these two exceptions applies, check the appropriate box and give the earlier registration number and date. Otherwise, do not submit Form VA; instead, write the Copyright Office for information about supplementary registration or recordation of transfers of copyright ownership.

Changed Version: If the work has been changed and you are now seeking registration to cover the additions or revisions, check the last box in space 5, give the earlier registration number and date, and complete both parts of space 6 in accordance with the instruction below.

Previous Registration Number and Date: If more than one previous registration has been made for the work, give the number and date of the latest registration.

6 SPACE 6: Derivative Work or Compilation

General Instructions: Complete space 6 if this work is a "changed version," "compilation," or "derivative work," and if it incorporates one or more earlier works that have already been published or registered for copyright, or that have fallen into the public domain. A "compilation" is defined as "a work formed by the collection and assembling of preexisting materials or of data that are selected, coordinated, or arranged in such a way that the resulting work as a whole constitutes an original work of authorship." A "derivative work" is "a work based on one or more preexisting works." Examples of derivative works include reproductions of works of art, sculptures based on drawings, lithographs based on paintings, maps based on previously published sources, or "any other form in which a work may be recast, transformed, or adapted." Derivative works also include works "consisting of editorial revisions, annotations, or other modifications" if these changes, as a whole, represent an original work of authorship.

Preexisting Material (space 6a): Complete this space *and* space 6b for derivative works. In this space identify the preexisting work that has been recast, transformed, or adapted. Examples of preexisting material might be "Grunewald Altarpiece" or "19th century quilt design." Do not complete this space for compilations.

Material Added to This Work (space 6b): Give a brief, general statement of the *additional* new material covered by the copyright claim for which registration is sought. In the case of a derivative work, identify this new material. Examples: "Adaptation of design and additional artistic work"; "Reproduction of painting by photolithography"; "Additional cartographic material"; "Compilation of photographs." If the work is a compilation, give a brief, general statement describing both the material that has been compiled *and* the compilation itself. Example: "Compilation of 19th century political cartoons."

7, 8, 9 SPACE 7, 8, 9: Fee, Correspondence, Certification, Return Address

Deposit Account: If you maintain a Deposit Account in the Copyright Office, identify it in space 7a. Otherwise, leave the space blank and send the fee with your application and deposit.

Correspondence (space 7b): Give the name, address, area code, telephone number, email address, and fax number (if available) of the person to be consulted if correspondence about this application becomes necessary.

Certification (space 8): The application cannot be accepted unless it bears the date and the *handwritten signature* of the author or other copyright claimant, or of the owner of exclusive right(s), or of the duly authorized agent of the author, claimant, or owner of exclusive right(s).

Address for Return of Certificate (space 9): The address box must be completed legibly since the certificate will be returned in a window envelope.

Copyright Office fees are subject to change.
For current fees, check the Copyright Office
website at *www.copyright.gov,* write the Copyright Office, or call (202) 707-3000.

Form VA
For a Work of the Visual Arts
UNITED STATES COPYRIGHT OFFICE

REGISTRATION NUMBER

	VA	VAU

EFFECTIVE DATE OF REGISTRATION

Month	Day	Year

DO NOT WRITE ABOVE THIS LINE. IF YOU NEED MORE SPACE, USE A SEPARATE CONTINUATION SHEET.

1

Title of This Work ▼   NATURE OF THIS WORK ▼ See instructions

Previous or Alternative Titles ▼

Publication as a Contribution If this work was published as a contribution to a periodical, serial, or collection, give information about the collective work in which the contribution appeared. **Title of Collective Work ▼**

If published in a periodical or serial give: **Volume ▼**   **Number ▼**   **Issue Date ▼**   **On Pages ▼**

2

a

NAME OF AUTHOR ▼   DATES OF BIRTH AND DEATH
                                                    Year Born ▼   Year Died ▼

Was this contribution to the work a   **Author's Nationality or Domicile**   Was This Author's Contribution to the Work
"work made for hire"?   Name of Country
  ☐ Yes   OR { Citizen of _____   Anonymous?   ☐ Yes ☐ No   If the answer to either
  ☐ No   Domiciled in _____   Pseudonymous?   ☐ Yes ☐ No   of these questions is
                                                                                                          "Yes," see detailed
                                                                                                          instructions.

Nature of Authorship Check appropriate box(es). **See instructions**
  ☐ 3-Dimensional sculpture   ☐ Map   ☐ Technical drawing
  ☐ 2-Dimensional artwork   ☐ Photograph   ☐ Text
  ☐ Reproduction of work of art   ☐ Jewelry design ☐ Architectural work

NOTE

Under the law, the "author" of a "work made for hire" is generally the employer, not the employee (see instructions). For any part of this work that was "made for hire" check "Yes" in the space provided, give the employer (or other person for whom the work was prepared) as "Author" of that part, and leave the space for dates of birth and death blank.

b

Name of Author ▼   Dates of Birth and Death
                                                    Year Born ▼   Year Died ▼

Was this contribution to the work a   **Author's Nationality or Domicile**   Was This Author's Contribution to the Work
"work made for hire"?   Name of Country
  ☐ Yes   OR { Citizen of _____   Anonymous?   ☐ Yes ☐ No   If the answer to either
  ☐ No   Domiciled in _____   Pseudonymous?   ☐ Yes ☐ No   of these questions is
                                                                                                          "Yes," see detailed
                                                                                                          instructions.

Nature of Authorship Check appropriate box(es). **See instructions**
  ☐ 3-Dimensional sculpture   ☐ Map   ☐ Technical drawing
  ☐ 2-Dimensional artwork   ☐ Photograph   ☐ Text
  ☐ Reproduction of work of art   ☐ Jewelry design ☐ Architectural work

3

a Year in Which Creation of This Work Was Completed   **b** Date and Nation of First Publication of This Particular Work
                                                                 Complete this information Month _____ Day _____ Year _____
      _____ Year This information must be given in all cases.   ONLY if this work has been published.   Nation

4

COPYRIGHT CLAIMANT(S) Name and address must be given even if the claimant is the same as the author given in space 2. ▼

See instructions before completing this space.

Transfer If the claimant(s) named here in space 4 is (are) different from the author(s) named in space 2, give a brief statement of how the claimant(s) obtained ownership of the copyright. ▼

DO NOT WRITE HERE OFFICE USE ONLY

APPLICATION RECEIVED

ONE DEPOSIT RECEIVED

TWO DEPOSITS RECEIVED

FUNDS RECEIVED

MORE ON BACK ▶   • Complete all applicable spaces (numbers 5-9) on the reverse side of this page.
                      • See detailed instructions.   • Sign the form at line 8.

DO NOT WRITE HERE

Page 1 of _____ pages

Form VA

EXAMINED BY	FORM VA
CHECKED BY	
☐ CORRESPONDENCE Yes	FOR COPYRIGHT OFFICE USE ONLY

DO NOT WRITE ABOVE THIS LINE. IF YOU NEED MORE SPACE, USE A SEPARATE CONTINUATION SHEET.

PREVIOUS REGISTRATION Has registration for this work, or for an earlier version of this work, already been made in the Copyright Office?

☐ Yes ☐ No If your answer is "Yes," why is another registration being sought? (Check appropriate box.) ▼

a. ☐ This is the first published edition of a work previously registered in unpublished form.

b. ☐ This is the first application submitted by this author as copyright claimant.

c. ☐ This is a changed version of the work, as shown by space 6 on this application.

If your answer is "Yes," give: **Previous Registration Number** ▼   **Year of Registration** ▼

5

DERIVATIVE WORK OR COMPILATION Complete both space 6a and 6b for a derivative work; complete only 6b for a compilation.

a. Preexisting Material Identify any preexisting work or works that this work is based on or incorporates. ▼

6
a

See instructions before completing this space.

b. Material Added to This Work Give a brief, general statement of the material that has been added to this work and in which copyright is claimed. ▼

b

DEPOSIT ACCOUNT If the registration fee is to be charged to a Deposit Account established in the Copyright Office, give name and number of Account.

Name ▼   **Account Number** ▼

7
a

CORRESPONDENCE Give name and address to which correspondence about this application should be sent. Name/Address/Apt/City/State/Zip ▼

b

Area code and daytime telephone number   (   )   Fax number   (   )

Email

CERTIFICATION* I, the undersigned, hereby certify that I am the

check only one ▶ {
☐ author
☐ other copyright claimant
☐ owner of exclusive right(s)
☐ authorized agent of _____
          Name of author or other copyright claimant, or owner of exclusive right(s) ▲

8

of the work identified in this application and that the statements made by me in this application are correct to the best of my knowledge.

Typed or printed name and date ▼ If this application gives a date of publication in space 3, do not sign and submit it before that date.

_____   Date _____

Handwritten signature (X) ▼

X _____

Certificate will be mailed in window envelope to this address:

Name ▼

Number/Street/Apt ▼

City/State/ZIP ▼

9

YOU MUST:
• Complete all necessary spaces
• Sign your application in space 8
SEND ALL 3 ELEMENTS IN THE SAME PACKAGE:
1. Application form
2. Nonrefundable filing fee in check or money order payable to *Register of Copyrights*
3. Deposit material
MAIL TO:
Library of Congress
Copyright Office
101 Independence Avenue SE
Washington, DC 20559-6000

*17 *USC* §506(e): Any person who knowingly makes a false representation of a material fact in the application for copyright registration provided for by section 409, or in any written statement filed in connection with the application, shall be fined not more than $2,500.

Form VA – Full   Rev: 07/2006   Print: 07/2006 – 30,000   Printed on recycled paper

U.S. Government Printing Office: 2004-320-958/60,125

Instructions for Short Form VA

For pictorial, graphic, and sculptural works

USE THIS FORM IF—

1. You are the *only* author and copyright owner of this work, *and*
2. The work was *not* made for hire, *and*
3. The work is completely new (does not contain a substantial amount of material that has been previously published or registered or is in the public domain).

If any of the above does not apply, you must use standard Form VA.

NOTE: *Short Form VA is not appropriate for an anonymous author who does not wish to reveal his or her identity.*

HOW TO COMPLETE SHORT FORM VA

- Type or print in black ink.
- Be clear and legible. (Your certificate of registration will be copied from your form.)
- Give only the information requested.

Note: You may use a continuation sheet (Form __/CON) to list individual titles in a collection. Complete Space A and list the individual titles under Space C on the back page. Space B is not applicable to short forms.

1 Title of This Work

You must give a title. If there is no title, state "UNTITLED." If you are registering an unpublished collection, give the collection title you want to appear in our records (for example: "Jewelry by Josephine, 1995 Volume"). Alternative title: If the work is known by two titles, you also may give the second title. If the work has been published as part of a larger work (including a periodical), give the title of that larger work instead of an alternative title, in addition to the title of the contribution.

2 Name and Address of Author and Owner of the Copyright

Give your name and mailing address. You may include your pseudonym followed by "pseud." Also, give the nation of which you are a citizen or where you have your domicile (i.e., permanent residence).
Give daytime phone and fax numbers and email address, if available.

3 Year of Creation

Give the latest year in which you completed the work you are registering at this time. A work is "created" when it is "fixed" in a tangible form. Examples: drawn on paper, molded in clay, stored in a computer.

4 Publication

If the work has been published (i.e., if copies have been distributed to the public), give the complete date of publication (month, day, and year) and the nation where the publication first took place.

5 Type of Authorship in This Work

Check the box or boxes that describe your authorship in the material you are sending. For example, if you are registering illustrations but have not written the story yet, check only the box for "2-dimensional artwork."

6 Signature of Author

Sign the application in black ink and check the appropriate box. The person signing the application should be the author or his/her authorized agent.

7 Person to Contact for Rights/Permissions

This space is optional. You may give the name and address of the person or organization to contact for permission to use the work. You may also provide phone, fax, or email information.

8 Certificate Will Be Mailed

This space must be completed. Your certificate of registration will be mailed in a window envelope to this address. Also, if the Copyright Office needs to contact you, we will write to this address.

9 Deposit Account

Complete this space only if you currently maintain a deposit account in the Copyright Office.

═══════════════ MAIL WITH THE FORM ═══════════════

- The filing fee in the form of a check or money order (*no cash*) payable to *Register of Copyrights.* (Copyright Office fees are subject to change. For current fees, check the Copyright Office website at *www.copyright.gov*, write the Copyright Office, or call (202) 707-3000.) — *and*

- One or two copies of the work or identifying material consisting of photographs or drawings showing the work. See table (right) for requirements for most works. **Note:** Request Circular 40a for information about the requirements for other works. Copies submitted become the property of the U.S. Government.

Mail everything (application form, copy or copies, and fee) *in one package* to:

Library of Congress
Copyright Office
101 Independence Avenue SE
Washington, DC 20559-6000

Questions? Call (202) 707-3000 [TTY: (202) 707-6737] between 8:30 a.m. and 5:00 p.m. eastern time, Monday through Friday except federal holidays. For forms and informational circulars, call (202) 707-9100 24 hours a day, 7 days a week, or download them from the Copyright Office website at *www.copyright.gov.*

If you are registering:	And the work is *unpublished/published* send:
• 2-dimensional artwork in a book, map, poster, or print	a. And the work is *unpublished*, send one complete copy or identifying material b. And the work is *published*, send two copies of the best published edition
• 3-dimensional sculpture, • 2-dimensional artwork applied to a T-shirt	a. And the work is *unpublished*, send identifying material b. And the work is *published*, send identifying material
• a greeting card, pattern, commercial print or label, fabric, wallpaper	a. And the work is *unpublished*, send one complete copy or identifying material b. And the work is *published*, send one copy of the best published edition

Form VA (Short Form)

Copyright Office fees are subject to change. For current fees, check the Copyright Office website at *www.copyright.gov,* write the Copyright Office, or call (202) 707-3000.

Short Form VA
For a Work of the Visual Arts
UNITED STATES COPYRIGHT OFFICE

REGISTRATION NUMBER

VA   VAU

Effective Date of Registration

Application Received

Examined By

Deposit Received
One   Two

Correspondence □   Fee Received

TYPE OR PRINT IN BLACK INK. DO NOT WRITE ABOVE THIS LINE.

1 **Title of This Work:**

Alternative title or title of larger work in which this work was published:

2 **Name and Address of Author and Owner of the Copyright:**

Nationality or domicile: Phone, fax, and email:

Phone (   )   Fax (   )
Email

3 **Year of Creation:**

4 **If work has been published, Date and Nation of Publication:**

a. Date _____ _____ _____ *(Month, day, and year all required)*
          Month   Day   Year

b. Nation

5 **Type of Authorship in This Work:** Check all that this author created.

❑ 3-Dimensional sculpture   ❑ Photograph   ❑ Map
❑ 2-Dimensional artwork   ❑ Jewelry design ❑ Text
❑ Technical drawing

6 **Signature:**

Registration cannot be completed without a signature.

*I certify that the statements made by me in this application are correct to the best of my knowledge.** Check one:

❑ Author ❑ Authorized agent

X _____

7 **Name and Address of Person to Contact for Rights and Permissions:** Phone, fax, and email:

OPTIONAL

❑ Check here if same as #2 above.

Phone (   )   Fax (   )
Email

8
Certificate will be mailed in window envelope to this address:

Name ▼

Number/Street/Apt ▼

City/State/ZIP ▼

Complete this space only if you currently hold a Deposit Account in the Copyright Office.

9 Deposit Account # _____
Name _____
_____
_____

DO NOT WRITE HERE   Page 1 of _____ pages

*17 *USC* §506(e): Any person who knowingly makes a false representation of a material fact in the application for copyright registration provided for by section 409, or in any written statement filed in connection with the application, shall be fined not more than $2,500.

Form VA-Short   Rev: 07/2006   Print: 07/2006 — 30,000   Printed on recycled paper

U.S. Government Printing Office: 2005-320-958/60,126

Adjunct Application Form GR/CP

Detach and read these instructions before completing this form.
Make sure all applicable spaces have been filled in before you return this form.

When to Use This Form

Use Form GR/CP when you are submitting a basic application on Form TX, Form PA, or Form VA for a group of works that qualify for a single registration under section 408(c)(2) of the copyright statute.

This Form:

- Is used solely as an adjunct to a basic application for copyright registration.
- Is not acceptable unless submitted with Form TX, Form PA, or Form VA.
- Is acceptable only if the group of works listed on it all qualify for a single copyright registration under 17 *USC* §408 (c)(2).

When Does a Group of Works Qualify for a Single Registration Under 17 *USC* §408(c)(2)?

For all works first published on or after March 1, 1989, a single copyright registration for a group of works can be made if *all* the following conditions are met:

1 All the works are by the same author, who is an individual (not an employer for hire); and

2 All the works were first published as contributions to periodicals (including newspapers) within a 12-month period; and

3 All the works have the same copyright claimant; and

4 The deposit accompanying the application consists of one copy of the entire periodical issue or newspaper section in which each contribution was first published; or a photocopy of the contribution itself; or a photocopy of the entire page containing the contribution; or the entire page containing the contribution cut or torn from the collective work; or the contribution cut or torn from the collective work; or photographs or photographic slides of the contribution or entire page containing the contribution as long as all contents of the contributions are clear and legible; and

5 The application identifies each contribution separately, including the periodical containing it and the date of its first publication.

> **Note:** For contributions that were first published prior to March 1, 1989, in addition to the conditions listed above, each contribution as first published must have borne a separate copyright notice, and the name of the owner of copyright in the work (or an abbreviation or alternative designation of the owner) must have been the same in each notice.

How to Apply for Group Registration

1 Study the information on this page to make sure that all the works you want to register together as a group qualify for a single registration.

2 Read through the procedure for group registration in the next column. Decide which form you should use for the basic registration. Be sure to have all the information you need before filling out both the basic and the adjunct application forms.

3 Complete the basic application form, following the detailed instructions accompanying it *and the special instructions on the reverse of this page.*

4 Complete the adjunct application on Form GR/CP and mail it, together with the basic application form, the fee, and the required copy of each contribution, to: *Library of Congress, Copyright Office, 101 Independence Avenue SE, Washington, DC 20559-6000*

Unless you have a Deposit Account in the Copyright Office, send a check or money order payable to *Register of Copyrights.*

Procedure for Group Registration

Two Application Forms Must Be Filed When you apply for a single registration to cover a group of contributions to periodicals, you must submit two application forms:

1 A basic application on either Form TX, Form PA, or Form VA. It must contain all the information required for copyright registration except the titles and information concerning publication of the contributions.

2 An adjunct application on Form GR/CP. This form provides separate identification for each contribution and gives information about first publication, as required by the statute.

Which Basic Application Form to Submit The basic application form you choose should be determined by the nature of the contributions you are registering. If they meet the statutory qualifications for group registration (outlined above), the contributions can be registered together even if they are entirely different in nature, type, or content. However, you must choose which of three forms is generally the most appropriate on which to submit your basic application:

- Form TX for nondramatic literary works consisting primarily of text. Examples are fiction, verse, articles, news stories, features, essays, reviews, editorials, columns, quizzes, puzzles, and advertising copy.

- Form PA for works of the performing arts. Examples are music, drama, choreography, and pantomimes.

- Form VA for works of the visual arts. Examples are photographs, drawings, paintings, prints, art reproductions, cartoons, comic strips, charts, diagrams, maps, pictorial ornamentation, and pictorial or graphic material published as advertising.

If your contributions differ in nature, choose the form most suitable for the majority of them.

Registration Fee for Group Registration Unless you maintain a deposit account in the Copyright Office, the registration fee must accompany your application forms and copies. Make your remittance payable to *Register of Copyrights.* Copyright Office fees are subject to change. For current fees, check the Copyright Office website at *www.copyright.gov,* write the Copyright Office, or call (202) 707-3000.

ISSN If a published serial has not been assigned an ISSN, application forms and additional information may be obtained from *Library of Congress, National Serials Data Program, Serial Record Division, Washington, DC 20540-4160.* Call (202) 707-6452. Or obtain information at *www.loc.gov/issn.*

What Copies Should Be Deposited for Group Registration? The application forms you file for group registration must be accompanied by one complete copy of each published contribution listed on Form GR/CP. For a description of acceptable deposits, see (4) under "When Does a Group of Works Qualify for a Single Registration under 17 *USC* §408(c)(2)?"

> **Note:** Since these deposit alternatives differ from the current regulations, the Office will automatically grant special relief upon receipt. There is no need for the applicant to request such relief in writing. This is being done to facilitate registration pending a change in the regulations.

The Copyright Notice: Before March 1, 1989, the use of a copyright notice was mandatory on all published works, and any work first published before that date should have carried a notice. Furthermore, among the conditions for group registration of contributions to periodicals for works first published prior to March 1, 1989, the statute establishes two requirements involving the copyright notice: (1) Each of the contributions as first published must have borne a

continued ▶

Form GR/CP

separate copyright notice; and (2) "The name of the owner of copyright in the works, or an abbreviation by which the name can be recognized, or a generally known alternative designation of the owner" must have been the same in each notice. For works first published on and after March 1, 1989, use of the copyright notice is optional. For more information about copyright notice, request Circular 3, *Copyright Notice.*

For Further Information: To speak to a Copyright Office staff member, call (202) 707-3000 (TTY: (202) 707-6737). Recorded information is available 24 hours a day. Order forms and other publications from *Library of Congress, Copyright Office, 101 Independence Avenue SE, Washington, DC 20559-6000* or call the Forms and Publications Hotline at (202) 707-9100. Access and download circulars, forms, and other information from the Copyright Office website at *www.copyright.gov.*

Note: The advantage of group registration is that it allows any number of works published within a 12-month period to be registered "on the basis of a single deposit, application, and registration fee." On the other hand, group registration may also have disadvantages under certain circumstances. If infringement of a published work begins before the work has been registered, the copyright owner can still obtain the ordinary remedies for copyright infringement (including injunctions, actual damages and profits, and impounding and disposition of infringing articles). However, in that situation—where the copyright in a published work is infringed before registration is made—the owner cannot obtain special remedies (statutory damages and attorney's fees) unless registration was made within 3 months after first publication of the work.

INSTRUCTIONS FOR THE BASIC APPLICATION FOR GROUP REGISTRATION

In general, the instructions for filling out the basic application (Form TX, Form PA, or Form VA) apply to group registrations. In addition, please observe the following specific instructions:

1 SPACE 1: Title

Do not give information concerning any of the contributions in space 1 of the basic application. Instead, in the block headed "Title of this Work," state: "See Form GR/CP, attached." Leave the other blocks in space 1 blank.

2 SPACE 2: Author

Give the name and other information concerning the author of all of the contributions listed in Form GR/CP. To qualify for group registration, all of the contributions must have been written by the same individual author.

3 SPACE 3: Creation and Publication

In the block calling for the year of creation, give the year of creation of the last of the contributions to be completed. Leave the block calling for the date and nation of first publication blank.

4 SPACE 4: Claimant

Give all of the requested information, which must be the same for all of the contributions listed on Form GR/CP.

Other Spaces

Complete all of the applicable spaces and be sure that the form is signed in the certification space.

HOW TO FILL OUT FORM GR/CP

Please type or print using black ink.

A PART A: Identification of Application

Identification of Basic Application: Indicate, by checking one of the boxes, which of the basic application forms (Form TX, Form PA, or Form VA) you are filing for registration.

Identification of Author and Claimant: Give the name of the individual author exactly as it appears in line 2 of the basic application, and give the name of the copyright claimant exactly as it appears in line 4. These must be the same for all of the contributions listed in Part B of Form GR/CP.

B PART B: Registration for Group of Contributions

General Instructions: Under the statute, a group of contributions to periodicals will qualify for a single registration only if the application "identifies each work separately, including the periodical containing it and its date of first publication." Part B of the Form GR/CP provides enough lines to list 19 separate contributions; if you need more space, use additional Forms GR/CP. If possible, list the contributions in the order of their publication, giving the earliest first. Number each line consecutively.

Important: All of the contributions listed on Form GR/CP must have been published within a single 12-month period. This does not mean that all of the contributions must have been published during the same calendar year, but it does mean that, to be grouped in a single application, the earliest and latest contributions must not have been published more than 12 months apart.

Example: Contributions published on April 1, 1978, July 1, 1978, and March 1, 1979, could be grouped together, but a contribution published on April 15, 1979, could not be registered with them as part of the group.

Title of Contribution: Each contribution must be given a title that identifies that particular work and can distinguish it from others. If the contribution as published in the periodical bears a title (or an identifying phrase that could serve as a title), transcribe its wording completely and exactly.

Identification of Periodical: Give the overall title of the periodical in which the contribution was first published, together with the volume and issue number (if any) and the issue date.

Pages: Give the number of the page of the periodical issue on which the contribution appeared. If the contribution covered more than one page, give the inclusive pages, if possible.

First Publication: The statute defines "publication" as "the distribution of copies or phonorecords of a work to the public by sale or other transfer of ownership, or by rental, lease, or lending"; a work is also "published" if there has been an "offering to distribute copies or phonorecords to a group of persons for purposes of further distribution, public performance, or public display." Give the full date (month, day, and year) when, and the country where, publication of the periodical issue containing the contribution first occurred. If first publication took place simultaneously in the United States and other countries, it is sufficient to state "U.S.A."

Form GR/CP

ADJUNCT APPLICATION
for Copyright Registration for a
Group of Contributions to Periodicals

- Use this adjunct form only if you are making a single registration for a group of contributions to periodicals, and you are also filing a basic application on Form TX, Form PA, or Form VA. Follow the instructions, attached.
- Number each line in Part B consecutively. Use additional Forms GR/CP if you need more space.
- Submit this adjunct form with the basic application form. Clip (do not tape or staple) and fold all sheets together before submitting them.
- **Copyright Office fees are subject to change. For current fees, check the Copyright Office website at** *www.copyright.gov,* **write the Coyright Office, or call (202) 707-3000.**

Ⓒ Form GR/CP
UNITED STATES COPYRIGHT OFFICE

REGISTRATION NUMBER

TX   PA   VA
EFFECTIVE DATE OF REGISTRATION

Month   Day   Year
FORM GR/CP RECEIVED

Page _____ of _____ pages

DO NOT WRITE ABOVE THIS LINE. FOR COPYRIGHT OFFICE USE ONLY

A
Identification
of
Application

IDENTIFICATION OF BASIC APPLICATION:
This application for copyright registration for a group of contributions to periodicals is submitted as an adjunct to an application filed on: (Check which)

☐ Form TX   ☐ Form PA   ☐ Form VA

IDENTIFICATION OF AUTHOR AND CLAIMANT: Give the name of the author and the name of the copyright claimant in all of the contributions listed in Part B of this form. The names should be the same as the names given in spaces 2 and 4 of the basic application.
Name of Author _____
Name of Copyright Claimant _____

B
Registration
for Group of
Contributions

COPYRIGHT REGISTRATION FOR A GROUP OF CONTRIBUTIONS TO PERIODICALS: To make a single registration for a group of works by the same individual author, all first published as contributions to periodicals within a 12-month period (see instructions), give full information about each contribution. If more space is needed, use additional Forms GR/CP.

☐ Title of Contribution _____
Title of Periodical _____ Vol.____ No._____ Issue Date _____ Pages _____
Date of First Publication _____ Nation of First Publication _____
(Month)   (Day)   (Year)   (Country)

☐ Title of Contribution _____
Title of Periodical _____ Vol.____ No._____ Issue Date _____ Pages _____
Date of First Publication _____ Nation of First Publication _____
(Month)   (Day)   (Year)   (Country)

☐ Title of Contribution _____
Title of Periodical _____ Vol.____ No._____ Issue Date _____ Pages _____
Date of First Publication _____ Nation of First Publication _____
(Month)   (Day)   (Year)   (Country)

☐ Title of Contribution _____
Title of Periodical _____ Vol.____ No._____ Issue Date _____ Pages _____
Date of First Publication _____ Nation of First Publication _____
(Month)   (Day)   (Year)   (Country)

☐ Title of Contribution _____
Title of Periodical _____ Vol.____ No._____ Issue Date _____ Pages _____
Date of First Publication _____ Nation of First Publication _____
(Month)   (Day)   (Year)   (Country)

☐ Title of Contribution _____
Title of Periodical _____ Vol.____ No._____ Issue Date _____ Pages _____
Date of First Publication _____ Nation of First Publication _____
(Month)   (Day)   (Year)   (Country)

☐ Title of Contribution _____
Title of Periodical _____ Vol.____ No._____ Issue Date _____ Pages _____
Date of First Publication _____ Nation of First Publication _____
(Month)   (Day)   (Year)   (Country)

Form GR/CP

FORM GR/CP

DO NOT WRITE ABOVE THIS LINE. FOR COPYRIGHT OFFICE USE ONLY.

☐ Title of Contribution _____
Title of Periodical _____ Vol.____ No._____ Issue Date _____ Pages _____
Date of First Publication _____ Nation of First Publication _____
(Month)   (Day)   (Year)   (Country)

B

Continued

☐ Title of Contribution _____
Title of Periodical _____ Vol.____ No._____ Issue Date _____ Pages _____
Date of First Publication _____ Nation of First Publication _____
(Month)   (Day)   (Year)   (Country)

☐ Title of Contribution _____
Title of Periodical _____ Vol.____ No._____ Issue Date _____ Pages _____
Date of First Publication _____ Nation of First Publication _____
(Month)   (Day)   (Year)   (Country)

☐ Title of Contribution _____
Title of Periodical _____ Vol.____ No._____ Issue Date _____ Pages _____
Date of First Publication _____ Nation of First Publication _____
(Month)   (Day)   (Year)   (Country)

☐ Title of Contribution _____
Title of Periodical _____ Vol.____ No._____ Issue Date _____ Pages _____
Date of First Publication _____ Nation of First Publication _____
(Month)   (Day)   (Year)   (Country)

☐ Title of Contribution _____
Title of Periodical _____ Vol.____ No._____ Issue Date _____ Pages _____
Date of First Publication _____ Nation of First Publication _____
(Month)   (Day)   (Year)   (Country)

☐ Title of Contribution _____
Title of Periodical _____ Vol.____ No._____ Issue Date _____ Pages _____
Date of First Publication _____ Nation of First Publication _____
(Month)   (Day)   (Year)   (Country)

☐ Title of Contribution _____
Title of Periodical _____ Vol.____ No._____ Issue Date _____ Pages _____
Date of First Publication _____ Nation of First Publication _____
(Month)   (Day)   (Year)   (Country)

☐ Title of Contribution _____
Title of Periodical _____ Vol.____ No._____ Issue Date _____ Pages _____
Date of First Publication _____ Nation of First Publication _____
(Month)   (Day)   (Year)   (Country)

☐ Title of Contribution _____
Title of Periodical _____ Vol.____ No._____ Issue Date _____ Pages _____
Date of First Publication _____ Nation of First Publication _____
(Month)   (Day)   (Year)   (Country)

☐ Title of Contribution _____
Title of Periodical _____ Vol.____ No._____ Issue Date _____ Pages _____
Date of First Publication _____ Nation of First Publication _____
(Month)   (Day)   (Year)   (Country)

☐ Title of Contribution _____
Title of Periodical _____ Vol.____ No._____ Issue Date _____ Pages _____
Date of First Publication _____ Nation of First Publication _____
(Month)   (Day)   (Year)   (Country)

United States Copyright Office

Circular 38a

International Copyright Relations of the United States

GENERAL INFORMATION

This circular sets forth U.S. copyright relations of current interest with the other independent nations of the world. Each entry gives country name (and alternate name) and a statement of copyright relations. The following code is used:

BAC   Party to the Buenos Aires Convention of 1910, as of the date given. U.S. ratification deposited with the Government of Argentina, May 1, 1911; proclaimed by the President of the United States, July 13, 1914.

Berne   Party to the Berne Convention for the Protection of Literary and Artistic Works as of the date given. Appearing within parentheses is the latest Act1 of the Convention to which the country is party. The effective date for the United States is March 1, 1989. The latest Act of the Convention, to which the United States is party, is the revision done at Paris on July 24, 1971.

Bilateral   Bilateral copyright relations with the United States by virtue of a proclamation or treaty, as of the date given. Where there is more than one proclamation or treaty, only the date of the first one is given.

None   No copyright relations with the United States.

Phonograms   Party to the Convention for the Protection of Producers of Phonograms Against Unauthorized Duplication of Their Phonograms, Geneva, 1971, as of the date given. The effective date for the United States is March 10, 1974.

SAT   Party to the Convention Relating to the Distribution of PROGRAMME-Carrying Signals Transmitted by Satellite, Brussels, 1974, as of the date given. The effective date for the United States is March 7, 1985.

UCC Geneva   Party to the Universal Copyright Convention, Geneva, 1952, as of the date given. The effective date for the United States is September 16, 1955.

UCC Paris   Party to the Universal Copyright Convention as revised at Paris, 1971, as of the date given. The effective date for the United States is July 10, 1974.

Unclear   Became independent since 1943. Has not established copyright relations with the United States, but may be honoring obligations incurred under former political status.

WCT   Party to the World Intellectual Property Organization Copyright Treaty, Geneva, 1996, as of the date provided. The effective date for the United States is March 6, 2002, the date the treaty entered into force.

WPPT   Party to the World Intellectual Property Organization Performances and Phonograms Treaty, Geneva, 1996, as of the date provided. The effective date for the United States if may 20, 2002, the date the treaty entered into force.

WTO   Member of the World Trade Organization (WTO), established pursuant to the Marrakesh Agreement of April 15, 1994, to implement the Uruguay Round Agreements. These Agreements affect, among other things, intangible property rights, including copyright and other intellectual property rights. The effective date of United States membership in the WTO is January 1, 1995. A country's membership in the WTO is effective as of the date indicated.

Circular 38a

RELATIONS AS OF JANUARY 2003

Afghanistan
None
Albania
Berne March 6, 1994 (Paris)[1]
WTO Sept. 8, 2000
WPPT May 20, 2002
Algeria
UCC Geneva Aug. 28, 1973
UCC Paris July 10, 1974
Berne April 19, 1998 (Paris)
Andorra
UCC Geneva Sept. 16, 1955
Angola
WTO Nov. 23, 1996
Antigua and Barbuda
WTO Jan. 1, 1995
Berne March 17, 2000 (Paris)
Argentina
Bilateral Aug. 23, 1934
BAC April 19, 1950
UCC Geneva Feb. 13, 1958
Berne June 10, 1967 (Paris)[2]
Phonograms June 30, 1973 3
WTO Jan. 1, 1995
WCT March 6, 2002
WPPT May 20, 2002
Armenia[17]
UCC Geneva May 27, 1973
SAT Dec.13, 1993
Berne Oct. 19, 2000 (Paris)
Australia
Bilateral March 15, 1918
Berne April 14, 1928 (Paris)[2]
UCC Geneva May 1, 1969
Phonograms June 22, 1974
UCC Paris Feb. 28, 1978
SAT Oct. 26,1990
WTO Jan. 1, 1995
Austria
Bilateral Sept. 20, 1907
Berne Oct. 1, 1920 (Paris)[2]
UCC Geneva July 2, 1957
SAT Aug. 6, 1982 4
UCC Paris Aug. 14, 1982
Phonograms Aug. 21, 1982
WTO Jan. 1, 1995
Azerbaijan[17]
UCC Geneva May 27, 1973
Berne June 4, 1999 (Paris)
Phonograms Sept. 1, 2001
Bahamas, The
Berne July 10, 1973 (Brussels)
UCC Geneva Dec. 27, 1976
UCC Paris Dec. 27, 1976

Bahrain
WTO Jan. 1, 1995
Berne March 2, 1997 (Paris)
Bangladesh
UCC Geneva Aug. 5, 1975
UCC Paris Aug. 5, 1975
WTO Jan. 1, 1995
Berne May 4, 1999 (Paris)
Barbados
UCC Geneva June 18, 1983
UCC Paris June 18, 1983
Berne July 30, 1983 (Paris)[2]
Phonograms July 29, 1983
WTO Jan. 1, 1995
Belarus[17]
UCC Geneva May 27, 1973
Berne Dec. 12, 1997 (Paris)
WCT March 6, 2002
WPPT May 20, 2002
Belgium
Berne Dec. 5, 1887 (Paris)[2]
Belize
UCC Geneva Dec. 1, 1982
WTO Jan. 1, 1995
Berne June 17, 2000 (Paris)
Benin
Berne Jan. 3, 1961 (Paris)[2]
WTO Feb. 22, 1996
Bhutan
None
Bolivia
BAC May 15, 1914
UCC Geneva March 22, 1990
UCC Paris March 22, 1990
Berne Nov. 4, 1993 (Paris)
WTO Sept. 12, 1995
Bosnia and Herzegovina
UCC Geneva May 11, 1966
UCC Paris July 10, 1974
Berne March 1, 1992 (Paris)
SAT March 6, 1992
Botswana
WTO May 31, 1995
Berne April 15, 1998 (Paris)
Brazil
BAC Aug. 31, 1915
Berne Feb. 9, 1922 (Paris)[2]
Bilateral April 2, 1957
UCC Geneva Jan. 13, 1960
Phonograms Nov. 28, 1975
UCC Paris Dec. 11, 1975
WTO Jan. 1, 1995
Brunei
WTO Jan. 1, 1995

Bulgaria
Berne Dec. 5, 1921 (Paris)[2]
UCC Geneva June 7, 1975
UCC Paris June 7, 1975
Phonograms Sept. 6, 1995
WTO Dec. 1, 1996
WCT March 6, 2002
WPPT May 20, 2002
Burkina Faso
Berne Aug. 19, 1963 (Paris)[2]
Phonograms Jan. 30, 1988
WTO June 3, 1995
WCT March 6, 2002
WPPT May 20, 2002
Burundi
WTO July 23, 1995
Cambodia
UCC Geneva Sept. 16, 1955
Cameroon
Berne Sept. 21, 1964 (Paris)[2]
UCC Geneva May 1, 1973
UCC Paris July 10, 1974
WTO Dec. 13, 1995
Canada
Bilateral Jan. 1, 1924
Berne April 10, 1928 (Paris)[2]
UCC Geneva Aug. 10, 1962
WTO Jan. 1, 1995
Cape Verde
Berne July 7, 1997 (Paris)
Central African Republic
Berne Sept. 3, 1977 (Paris)[2]
WTO May 31, 1995
Chad
Berne Nov. 25, 1971 (Brussels)[2]
WTO Oct. 19, 1996
Chile
Bilateral May 25, 1896
BAC June 14, 1955
UCC Geneva Sept. 16, 1955
Berne June 5, 1970 (Paris)[2]
Phonograms March 24, 1977
WTO Jan. 1, 1995
WCT March 6, 2002
WPPT May 20, 2002
China
Bilateral Jan. 13, 1904[5]
Bilateral March 17, 1992[9]
Berne Oct. 15, 1992 (Paris)
UCC Geneva Oct. 30, 1992
UCC Paris Oct. 30, 1992
Phonograms April 30, 1993
WTO Dec. 22, 2001

Explanations of footnotes appear on pages 8–9

Chinese Taipei
WTO Jan. 1, 2002
Colombia
BAC Dec. 23, 1936
UCC Geneva June 18, 1976
UCC Paris June 18, 1976
Berne March 7, 1988 (Paris)[2]
Phonograms May 16, 1994
WTO April 30, 1995
WCT March 6, 2002
WPPT May 20, 2002
Comoros
Unclear
Congo, Democratic Republic of the
Berne Oct. 8, 1963 (Paris)[2]
Phonograms Nov. 29, 1977
WTO Jan. 1, 1997
Congo, Republic of the
Berne May 8, 1962 (Paris)[2]
WTO March 27, 1997
Costa Rica[6]
Bilateral Oct. 19, 1899
BAC Nov. 30, 1916
UCC Geneva Sept. 16, 1955
Berne June 10, 1978 (Paris)[2]
UCC Paris March 7, 1980
Phonograms June 17, 1982
WTO Jan. 1, 1995
SAT June 25, 1999
WCT March 6, 2002
WPPT May 20, 2002
Cote d'Ivoire
Berne Jan. 1, 1962 (Paris)[2]
WTO Jan. 1, 1995
Croatia
UCC Geneva May 11, 1966
UCC Paris July 10, 1974
Berne Oct. 8, 1991 (Paris)[2]
SAT Oct. 8, 1991
Phonograms April 20, 2000
WTO Nov. 30, 2000
WCT March 6, 2002
WPPT May 20, 2002
Cuba
Bilateral Nov. 17, 1903
UCC Geneva June 18, 1957
WTO April 20, 1995
Berne Feb. 20, 1997 (Paris)
Cyprus
Berne Feb. 24, 1964 (Paris)[2]
UCC Geneva Dec. 19, 1990
UCC Paris Dec. 19,1990
Phonograms Sept. 30, 1993
WTO July 30, 1995

Czech Republic
UCC Geneva Jan. 6, 1960
UCC Paris April 17, 1980
Berne Jan. 1, 1993 (Paris)
Phonograms Jan. 1, 1993
WTO Jan. 1, 1995
WCT March 6, 2002
WPPT May 20, 2002
Denmark
Bilateral May 8, 1893
Berne July 1, 1903 (Paris)[2]
UCC Geneva Feb. 9, 1962
Phonograms March 24, 1977
UCC Paris July 11, 1979
WTO Jan. 1, 1995
Djibouti
WTO May 31, 1995
Berne May 13, 2002 (Paris)
Dominica
WTO Jan. 1, 1995
Berne Aug. 7, 1999 (Paris)
Dominican Republic[6]
BAC Oct. 31, 1912
UCC Geneva May 8, 1983
UCC Paris May 8, 1983
WTO March 9, 1995
Berne Dec. 24, 1997 (Paris)
Ecuador
BAC Aug. 31, 1914
UCC Geneva June 5, 1957
Phonograms Sept. 14, 1974
UCC Paris Sept. 6, 1991
Berne Oct. 9, 1991 (Paris)
WTO Jan. 21, 1996
WCT March 6, 2002
WPPT May 20, 2002
Egypt
Berne June 7, 1977 (Paris)[2]
Phonograms April 23, 1978
WTO June 30, 1995
El Salvador
Bilateral June 30, 1908, by virtue of
Mexico City Convention, 1902
Phonograms Feb. 9, 1979
UCC Geneva March 29, 1979
UCC Paris March 29, 1979
Berne Feb. 19, 1994 (Paris)
WTO May 7, 1995
WCT March 6, 2002
WPPT May 20, 2002
Equatorial Guinea
Berne June 26, 1997 (Paris)
Estonia
Berne Oct. 26, 1994 (Paris)
WTO Nov. 13, 1999
Phonograms May 28, 2000

Ethiopia
None
European Community
WTO Jan. 1, 1995
Fiji
Berne Dec.1, 1971 (Brussels)[2]
UCC Geneva March 13, 1972
Phonograms April. 18, 1973 3
WTO Jan. 14, 1996
Finland
Berne April 1, 1928 (Paris)[2]
Bilateral Jan. 1, 1929
UCC Geneva April 16, 1963
Phonograms April 18, 1973[3]
UCC Paris Nov. 1, 1986
WTO Jan. 1, 1995
France
Berne Dec. 5, 1887 (Paris)[2]
Bilateral July 1, 1891[14]
UCC Geneva Jan. 14, 1956
Phonograms April 18, 1973[3]
UCC Paris July 10, 1974
WTO Jan. 1, 1995
Gabon
Berne March 26, 1962 (Paris)[2]
WTO Jan. 1, 1995
WCT March 6, 2002
WPPT May 20, 2002
Gambia, The
Berne March 7, 1993 (Paris)
WTO Oct. 23, 1996
Georgia[17]
UCC Geneva May 27, 1973
Berne May 16, 1995 (Paris)
WTO June 14, 2000
WCT March 6, 2002
WPPT May 20, 2002
Germany[10, 15]
Berne Dec. 5, 1887 (Paris)[2, 7]
Bilateral April 15, 1892
UCC Geneva Sept. 16, 1955
Bilateral July 12, 1967[15]
Phonograms May 18, 1974
UCC Paris July 10, 1974
SAT Aug. 25, 1979[4]
WTO Jan. 1, 1995
Ghana
UCC Geneva Aug. 22, 1962
Berne Oct. 11, 1991 (Paris)
WTO Jan. 1, 1995
Greece
Berne Nov. 9, 1920 (Paris)[2]
Bilateral March 1, 1932
UCC Geneva Aug. 24, 1963
SAT Oct. 22, 1991
Phonograms Feb. 9, 1994
WTO Jan. 1, 1995

Grenada
WTO Feb. 22, 1996
Berne Sept. 22, 1998 (Paris)

Guatemala[6]
BAC March 28, 1913
UCC Geneva Oct. 28, 1964
Phonograms Feb. 1, 1977
WTO July 21, 1995
Berne July 28, 1997 (Paris)
WCT Feb. 4, 2003
WPPT Jan. 8, 2003

Guinea
Berne Nov. 20, 1980 (Paris)[2]
UCC Geneva Nov. 13, 1981
UCC Paris Nov. 13, 1981
WTO Oct. 25, 1995
WCT May 25, 2002
WPPT May 25, 2002

Guinea-Bissau
Berne July 22, 1991 (Paris)
WTO May 31, 1995

Guyana
Berne Oct. 25, 1994 (Paris)
WTO Jan. 1, 1995

Haiti
BAC Nov. 27, 1919
UCC Geneva Sept. 16, 1955
Berne Jan. 11, 1996 (Paris)
WTO Jan. 30, 1996

Honduras[6]
BAC April 27, 1914
Berne Jan. 25,1990 (Paris)
Phonograms March 6, 1990
WTO Jan. 1, 1995
WCT May 20, 2002
WPPT May 20, 2002

Hong Kong[12]
WTO Jan. 1, 1995
Berne July 1, 1997 (Paris)
Phonograms July 1, 1997

Hungary
Bilateral Oct. 16, 1912
Berne Feb. 14, 1922 (Paris)[2]
UCC Geneva Jan. 23, 1971
UCC Paris July 10, 1974
Phonograms May 28, 1975
WTO Jan. 1, 1995
WCT March 6, 2002
WPPT May 20, 2002

Iceland
Berne Sept. 7, 1947 (Rome)[2]
UCC Geneva Dec. 18, 1956
WTO Jan. 1, 1995

India
Berne April 1, 1928 (Paris)[2]
Bilateral Aug. 15, 1947
UCC Geneva Jan. 21, 1958
Phonograms Feb. 12, 1975
UCC Paris April 7, 1988
WTO Jan. 1, 1995

Indonesia
Bilateral Aug. 1, 1989
WTO Jan. 1, 1995
Berne Sept. 5, 1997 (Paris)
WCT March 6, 2002

Iran
None

Iraq
None

Ireland
Berne Oct. 5, 1927 (Brussels)[2]
Bilateral Oct. 1, 1929
UCC Geneva Jan. 20, 1959
WTO Jan. 1, 1995

Israel
Bilateral May 15, 1948
Berne March 24, 1950 (Brussels)[2]
UCC Geneva Sept. 16, 1955
Phonograms May 1, 1978
WTO April 21, 1995

Italy
Berne Dec. 5, 1887 (Paris)[2]
Bilateral Oct. 31, 1892
UCC Geneva Jan. 24, 1957
Phonograms March 24, 1977
UCC Paris Jan. 25, 1980
SAT July 7, 1981[4]
WTO Jan. 1, 1995

Jamaica
Berne Jan. 1, 1994 (Paris)
Phonograms Jan. 11, 1994
WTO March 9, 1995
SAT Jan. 12, 2000
WCT June 12, 2002
WPPT June 12, 2002

Japan[8]
Berne July 15, 1899 (Paris)[2]
UCC Geneva April 28, 1956
UCC Paris Oct. 21, 1977
Phonograms Oct. 14, 1978
WTO Jan. 1, 1995
WCT March 6, 2002
WPPT Oct. 9, 2002

Jordan
Berne July 28, 1999 (Paris)
WTO April 11, 2000
Bilateral Dec. 17, 2001[16]

Kazakhstan[17]
UCC Geneva May 27, 1973
Berne April 12, 1999 (Paris)
Phonograms Aug. 3, 2001

Kenya
UCC Geneva Sept. 7, 1966
UCC Paris July 10, 1974
Phonograms April 21, 1976
SAT Aug. 25, 1979[4]
Berne June 11, 1993 (Paris)
WTO Jan. 1, 1995

Kiribati
Unclear

Korea, North
Unclear

Korea, South
UCC Geneva Oct. 1, 1987
UCC Paris Oct. 1, 1987
Phonograms Oct. 10, 1987
WTO Jan. 1, 1995
Berne Aug. 21, 1996 (Paris)

Kuwait
WTO Jan. 1, 1995

Kyrgyz Republic[17]
UCC Geneva May 27, 1973
WTO Dec. 20, 1998
Berne July 8, 1999 (Paris)
WCT March 6, 2002
WPPT Aug. 15, 2002
Phonograms Oct. 12, 2002

Laos
UCC Geneva Sept. 16, 1955

Latvia
Berne Aug. 11, 1995 (Paris)
Phonograms Aug. 23, 1997
WTO Feb. 10, 1999
WCT March 6, 2002
WPPT May 20, 2002

Lebanon
Berne Sept. 30, 1947 (Rome)[2]
UCC Geneva Oct. 17, 1959

Lesotho
Berne Sept. 28, 1989 (Paris)
WTO May 31, 1995

Liberia
UCC Geneva July 27, 1956
Berne March 8, 1989 (Paris)

Libya
Berne Sept. 28, 1976 (Paris)[2]

Liechtenstein
Berne July 30, 1931 (Paris)[2]
UCC Geneva Jan. 22, 1959
WTO Sept. 1, 1995
Phonograms Oct. 12, 1999
UCC Paris Nov. 11, 1999

Explanations of footnotes appear on pages 8–9

Lithuania
Berne Dec. 14, 1994 (Paris)
Phonograms Jan. 27, 2000
WTO May 31, 2001
WCT March 6, 2002
WPPT May 20, 2002

Luxembourg
Berne June 20, 1888 (Paris)[2]
Bilateral June 29, 1910
UCC Geneva Oct. 15, 1955
Phonograms March 8, 1976
WTO Jan. 1, 1995

Macau
WTO Jan. 1, 1995
Berne Dec. 20, 1999 (Paris)

Macedonia
Berne Sept. 8, 1991 (Paris)
SAT Nov. 17, 1991
UCC Geneva July 30, 1997
UCC Paris July 30, 1997
Phonograms March 2, 1998

Madagascar
Berne Jan. 1, 1966 (Brussels)[2]
WTO Nov. 17, 1995

Malawi
UCC Geneva Oct. 26, 1965
Berne Oct. 12, 1991 (Paris)
WTO May 31, 1995

Malaysia
Berne Oct. 1, 1990 (Paris)
WTO Jan. 1, 1995

Maldives
WTO May 31, 1995

Mali
Berne March 19, 1962 (Paris)[2]
WTO May 31, 1995
WCT April 24, 2002
WPPT May 20, 2002

Malta
Berne Sept. 21, 1964 (Rome)[2]
UCC Geneva Nov. 19, 1968
WTO Jan. 1, 1995

Mauritania
Berne Feb. 6, 1973 (Paris)[2]
WTO May 31, 1995

Mauritius
UCC Geneva March 12, 1968
Berne May 10, 1989 (Paris)
WTO Jan. 1, 1995

Mexico
Bilateral Feb. 27, 1896
UCC Geneva May 12, 1957
BAC April 24, 1964
Berne June 11, 1967 (Paris)[2]
Phonograms Dec. 21, 1973[3]
UCC Paris Oct. 31, 1975
SAT Aug. 25, 1979[4]
WTO Jan. 1, 1995
WCT March 6, 2002
WPPT May 20, 2002

Moldova[17]
UCC Geneva May 27, 1973
Berne Nov. 2, 1995 (Paris)
Phonograms July 17, 2000
WTO July 26, 2001
WCT March 6, 2002
WPPT May 20, 2002

Monaco
Berne May 30, 1889 (Paris)[2]
Bilateral Oct. 15, 1952
UCC Geneva Sept. 16, 1955
Phonograms Dec. 2, 1974
UCC Paris Dec. 13, 1974

Mongolia
WTO Jan. 29, 1997
Berne March 12, 1998 (Paris)
WCT Oct. 25, 2002
WPPT Oct. 25, 2002

Morocco
Berne June 16, 1917 (Paris)[2]
UCC Geneva May 8, 1972
UCC Paris Jan. 28, 1976
SAT June 30, 1983[4]
WTO Jan. 1, 1995

Mozambique
WTO Aug. 26, 1995

Myanmar, Union of
WTO Jan. 1, 1995

Namibia
Berne March 21, 1990 (Paris)
WTO Jan. 1, 1995

Nauru
Unclear

Nepal
None

Netherlands and Possessions
Bilateral Nov. 20, 1899
Berne Nov. 1, 1912 (Paris)[2]
UCC Geneva June 22, 1967
UCC Paris Nov. 30, 1985
Phonograms Oct. 12, 1993
WTO Jan. 1, 1995

New Zealand
Bilateral Dec. 1, 1916
Berne April 24, 1928 (Rome)[2]
UCC Geneva Sept. 11, 1964
Phonograms Aug. 13, 1976
WTO Jan. 1, 1995

Nicaragua[6]
BAC Dec. 15, 1913
UCC Geneva Aug. 16, 1961
SAT Aug. 25, 1979[4]
WTO Sept. 3, 1995
Phonograms Aug. 10, 2000
Berne Aug. 23, 2000 (Paris)
WCT March 6, 2003
WPPT March 6, 2003

Niger
Berne May 2, 1962 (Paris)[2]
UCC Geneva May 15, 1989
UCC Paris May 15, 1989
WTO Dec. 13, 1996

Nigeria
UCC Geneva Feb. 14, 1962
Berne Sept. 14, 1993 (Paris)
WTO Jan. 1, 1995

Norway
Berne April 13, 1896 (Paris)[2]
Bilateral July 1, 1905
UCC Geneva Jan. 23, 1963
UCC Paris Aug. 7, 1974
Phonograms Aug. 1, 1978
WTO Jan. 1, 1995

Oman
Berne July 14, 1999 (Paris)
WTO Nov. 9, 2000

Pakistan
Berne July 5, 1948 (Rome)[2]
UCC Geneva Sept. 16, 1955
WTO Jan. 1, 1995

Palau
Unclear

Panama
BAC Nov. 25, 1913
UCC Geneva Oct. 17, 1962
Phonograms June 29, 1974
UCC Paris Sept. 3, 1980
SAT Sept. 25, 1985
Berne June 8, 1996 (Paris)
WTO Sept. 6, 1997
WCT March 6, 2002
WPPT May 20, 2002

Papua New Guinea
WTO June 9, 1996

Explanations of footnotes appear on pages 8–9

5

Paraguay
BAC Sept. 20, 1917
UCC Geneva March 11, 1962
Phonograms Feb. 13, 1979
Berne Jan. 2, 1992 (Paris)
WTO Jan. 1, 1995
WCT March 6, 2002
WPPT May 20, 2002

Peru
BAC April 30, 1920
UCC Geneva Oct. 16, 1963
UCC Paris July 22, 1985
SAT Aug. 7, 1985
Phonograms Aug. 24, 1985
Berne Aug. 20, 1988 (Paris)[2]
WTO Jan. 1, 1995
WCT March 6, 2002
WPPT July 18, 2002

Philippines
Bilateral Oct. 21, 1948
Berne Aug. 1, 1951 (Paris)[2]
WTO Jan. 1, 1995
WCT Oct. 4, 2002
WPPT Oct. 4, 2002

Poland
Berne Jan. 28, 1920 (Paris)[2]
Bilateral Feb. 16, 1927
UCC Geneva March 9, 1977
UCC Paris March 9, 1977
WTO July 1, 1995

Portugal
Bilateral July 20, 1893
Berne March 29, 1911 (Paris)[2]
UCC Geneva Dec. 25, 1956
UCC Paris July 30, 1981
WTO Jan. 1, 1995
SAT March 11, 1996

Qatar
WTO Jan. 13, 1996
Berne July 5, 2000 (Paris)

Romania
Berne Jan. 1, 1927 (Paris)[2]
Bilateral May 14, 1928
WTO Jan. 1, 1995
Phonograms Oct. 1, 1998
WCT March 6, 2002
WPPT May 20, 2002

Russia[17]
UCC Geneva May 27, 1973
SAT Dec. 25, 1991
UCC Paris March 9, 1995
Berne March 13, 1995 (Paris)
Phonograms March 13, 1995

Rwanda
Berne March 1, 1984 (Paris)[2]
UCC Geneva Nov. 10, 1989
UCC Paris Nov. 10, 1989
WTO May 22, 1996

St. Kitts and Nevis
Berne April 9, 1995 (Paris)[2]
WTO Feb. 21, 1996

Saint Lucia
Berne Aug. 24, 1993 (Paris)[2]
WTO Jan. 1, 1995
Phonograms April 2, 2001
WCT March 6, 2002
WPPT May 20, 2002

Saint Vincent and the Grenadines
UCC Geneva April 22, 1985
UCC Paris April 22, 1985
WTO Jan. 1, 1995
Berne Aug. 29, 1995 (Paris)

San Marino
None

São Tomé and Principe
Unclear

Saudi Arabia
UCC Geneva July 13, 1994
UCC Paris July 13, 1994

Senegal
Berne Aug. 25, 1962 (Paris)[2]
UCC Geneva July 9, 1974
UCC Paris July 10, 1974
WTO Jan. 1, 1995
WCT May 18, 2002
WPPT May 20, 2002

Serbia and Montenegro
Berne June 17, 1930 (Paris)[2]
UCC Geneva May 11, 1966
UCC Paris July 10, 1974
SAT Aug. 25, 1979 4

Seychelles
Unclear

Sierra Leone
WTO July 23, 1995

Singapore
Bilateral May 18, 1987
WTO Jan. 1, 1995
Berne Dec. 21, 1998 (Paris)

Slovakia
UCC Geneva Jan. 6, 1960
UCC Paris April 17, 1980
Berne Jan. 1, 1993 (Paris)[2]
Phonograms Jan. 1, 1993
WTO Jan. 1, 1995
WCT March 6, 2002
WPPT May 20, 2002

Slovenia
UCC Geneva May 11, 1966
UCC Paris July 10, 1974
Berne June 25, 1991 (Paris)[2]
SAT June 25, 1991
WTO July 30, 1995
Phonograms Oct. 15, 1996
WCT March 6, 2002
WPPT May 20, 2002

Solomon Islands
WTO July 26, 1996

Somalia
Unclear

South Africa
Bilateral July 1, 1924
Berne Oct. 3, 1928 (Brussels)[2]
WTO Jan. 1, 1995

Spain
Berne Dec. 5, 1887 (Paris)[2]
Bilateral July 10, 1895
UCC Geneva Sept. 16, 1955
UCC Paris July 10, 1974
Phonograms Aug. 24, 1974
WTO Jan. 1, 1995

Sri Lanka
Berne July 20, 1959 (Rome)[2]
UCC Geneva Jan. 25, 1984
UCC Paris Jan. 25, 1984
WTO Jan. 1, 1995

Sudan
Berne Dec. 28, 2000 (Paris)

Suriname
Berne Feb. 23, 1977 (Paris)[2]
WTO Jan. 1, 1995

Swaziland
WTO Jan. 1, 1995
Berne Dec. 14, 1998 (Paris)

Sweden
Berne Aug. 1, 1904 (Paris)[2]
Bilateral June 1, 1911
UCC Geneva July 1, 1961
Phonograms April 18, 1973[3]
UCC Paris July 10, 1974
WTO Jan. 1, 1995

Switzerland
Berne Dec. 5, 1887 (Paris)[2]
Bilateral July 1, 1891[14]
UCC Geneva March 30, 1956
UCC Paris Sept. 21, 1993
SAT Sept. 24, 1993
Phonograms Sept. 30, 1993
WTO July 1, 1995

Syria
Unclear

Explanations of footnotes appear on pages 8–9

Tajikistan[17]
　UCC Geneva May 27, 1973
　Berne March 9, 2000 (Paris)
Tanzania
　Berne July 25, 1994 (Paris)
　WTO Jan. 1, 1995
Thailand
　Bilateral Sept. 1, 1921
　Berne July 17, 1931 (Paris)[2]
　WTO Jan. 1, 1995
Togo
　Berne April 30, 1975 (Paris)[2]
　WTO May 31, 1995
Tonga
　Berne June 14, 2001 (Paris)
Trinidad and Tobago
　Berne Aug. 16, 1988 (Paris)[2]
　UCC Geneva Aug. 19, 1988
　UCC Paris Aug. 19, 1988
　Phonograms Oct. 1, 1988
　WTO March 1, 1995
　SAT Nov. 1, 1996
Tunisia
　Berne Dec. 5, 1887 (Paris)[2]
　UCC Geneva June 19, 1969
　UCC Paris June 10, 1975
　WTO March 29, 1995
Turkey
　Berne Jan. 1, 1952 (Paris)[2]
　WTO March 26, 1995

Turkmenistan[17]
　UCC Geneva May 27, 1973
Tuvalu
　Unclear
Uganda
　WTO Jan. 1, 1995
Ukraine[17]
　UCC Geneva May 27, 1973
　Berne Oct. 25, 1995 (Paris)
　Phonograms Feb. 18, 2000
　WCT March 6, 2002
　WPPT May 20, 2002
United Arab Emirates
　WTO April 10, 1996
United Kingdom
　Berne Dec. 5, 1887 (Paris)[2]
　Bilateral July 1, 1891[14]
　UCC Geneva Sept. 27, 1957
　Phonograms April 18, 1973[3]
　UCC Paris July 10, 1974
　WTO Jan. 1, 1995
Uruguay
　BAC Dec. 17, 1919
　Berne July 10, 1967 (Paris)[2]
　Phonograms Jan. 18, 1983
　UCC Geneva April 12, 1993
　UCC Paris April 12, 1993
　WTO Jan. 1, 1995
Uzbekistan[17]
　UCC Geneva May 27, 1973

Vanuatu
　Unclear
Vatican City
　Berne Sept. 12, 1935 (Paris)[2]
　UCC Geneva Oct. 5, 1955
　Phonograms July 18, 1977
　UCC Paris May 6, 1980
Venezuela
　UCC Geneva Sept. 30, 1966
　Phonograms Nov. 18, 1982
　Berne Dec. 30, 1982 (Paris)[2]
　WTO Jan. 1, 1995
　UCC Paris Feb. 11, 1997
Vietnam
　Bilateral Dec. 23, 1998[13]
　Bilateral Dec. 10, 2001
Yemen
　(Unclear)
Zambia
　UCC Geneva June 1, 1965
　Berne Jan. 2, 1992 (Paris)[2]
　WTO Jan. 1, 1995
Zimbabwe
　Berne April 18, 1980 (Rome)[2]
　WTO March 5, 1995

STATUTORY PROVISIONS

Reprinted below is section 104 of title 17 of the United States Code, as of March 1, 2003.

§ 104. Subject matter of copyright: National origin

(a) Unpublished Works.-The works specified by sections 102 and 103, while unpublished, are subject to protection under this title without regard to the nationality or domicile of the author.

(b) **Published Works.** The works specified by sections 102 and 103, when published, are subject to protection under this title if-

(1) on the date of first publication, one or more of the authors is a national or domiciliary of the United States, or is a national, domiciliary, or sovereign authority of a treaty party, or is a stateless person, wherever that person may be domiciled; or

(2) the work is first published in the United States or in a foreign nation that, on the date of first publication, is a treaty party; or

(3) the work is a sound recording that was first fixed in a treaty party; or

(4) the work is a pictorial, graphic, or sculptural work that is incorporated in a building or other structure, or an architectural work that is embodied in a building and the building or structure is located in the United States or a treaty party; or

(5) the work is first published by the United Nations or any of its specialized agencies, or by the Organization of American States; or

(6) the work comes within the scope of a Presidential proclamation. Whenever the President finds that a particular foreign nation extends, to works by authors who are nationals or domiciliaries of the United States or to works that are first published in the United States, copyright protection on substantially the same basis as that on which the foreign nation extends protection to works of its own nationals and domiciliaries and works first published in that nation, the President may by proclamation extend protection under this title to works of which one or more of the authors is, on the date of first publication, a national, domiciliary, or sovereign authority of that nation, or which was first published in that nation. The President may revise, suspend, or revoke any such proclamation or impose any conditions or limitations on protection under a proclamation.

For purposes of paragraph (2), a work that is published in the United States or a treaty party within 30 days after publication in a foreign nation that is not a treaty party shall be considered to be first published in the United States or such treaty party, as the case may be.

(c) **Effect of Berne Convention.** No right or interest in a work eligible for protection under this title may be claimed by virtue of, or in reliance upon, the provisions of the Berne Convention, or the adherence of the United States thereto. Any rights in a work eligible for protection under this title that derive from this title, other Federal or State statutes, or the common law, shall not be expanded or reduced by virtue of, or in reliance upon, the provisions of the Berne Convention, or the adherence of the United States thereto.

(d) Effect of Phonograms Treaties.-Notwithstanding the provisions of subsection (b), no works other than sound recordings shall be eligible for protection under this title solely by virtue of the adherence of the United States to the Geneva Phonograms Convention or the WIPO Performances and Phonograms Treaty.

SOME POINTS TO REMEMBER REGARDING THE INTERNATIONAL PROTECTION OF LITERARY AND ARTISTIC WORKS

There is no such thing as an "international copyright" that will automatically protect an author's writings throughout the world. Protection against unauthorized use in a particular country basically depends on the national laws of that country. However, most countries offer protection to foreign works under certain conditions that have been greatly simplified by international copyright treaties and conventions. There are two principal international copyright conventions, the Berne Union for the Protection of Literary and Artistic Property (Berne Convention) and the Universal Copyright Convention (UCC).

An author who wishes copyright protection for his or her work in a particular country should first determine the extent of the protection available to works of foreign authors in that country. If possible, this should be done before the work is published anywhere, because protection may depend on the facts existing at the time of first publication.

If the country in which protection is sought is a party to one of the international copyright conventions, the work generally may be protected by complying with the conditions of that convention. Even if the work cannot be brought under an international convention, protection under the specific provisions of the country's national laws may still be possible. There are, however, some countries that offer little or no copyright protection to any foreign works. For current information on the requirements and protection provided by other countries, it may be advisable to consult an expert familiar with foreign copyright laws. The U.S. Copyright Office is not permitted to recommend agents or attorneys or to give legal advice on foreign laws.

FOOTNOTES

[1] "Paris" means the Berne Convention for the Protection of Literary and Artistic Works as revised at Paris on July 24, 1971 (Paris Act)

"Stockholm" means the said Convention as revised at Stockholm on July 14, 1967 (Stockholm Act) "Brussels" means the said Convention as revised at Brussels on June 26, 1948 (Brussels Act) "Rome" means the said Convention as revised at Rome on June 2, 1928 (Rome Act)

"Berlin" means the said Convention as revised at Berlin on Nov. 13, 1908 (Berlin Act).

NOTE: In each case the reference to Act signifies adherence to the substantive provisions of such Act only, e.g., Articles 1 to 21 and the Appendix of the Paris Act. Articles 22 to 38 deal with administration and structure.

[2] The Berne Convention for the Protection of Literary and Artistic Works of Sept. 9, 1886, as revised at Paris on July 24, 1971, did not enter into force with respect to the United States until March 1, 1989.

[3] The Convention for the Protection of Producers of Phonograms Against Unauthorized Duplication of Their Phonograms done at Geneva on Oct. 29, 1971, did not enter into force with respect to the United States until March 10, 1974.

[4] The Convention Relating to the Distribution of Programme-Carrying Signals Transmitted by Satellite done at Brussels on May 21, 1974, did not enter into force with respect to the United States until March 7, 1985.

[5] The government of the People's Republic of China views this treaty as not binding on the PRC. In the territory administered by the authorities on Taiwan the treaty is considered to be in force.

[6] This country became a party to the Mexico City Convention, 1902, effective June 30, 1908, to which the United States also became a party, effective on the same date. As regards copyright relations with the United States, this Convention is considered to have been superseded by adherence of this country and the United States to the Buenos Aires Convention of 1910.

[7] Date on which the accession by the German Empire became effective.

[8] Bilateral copyright relations between Japan and the United States, which were formulated effective May 10, 1906, are considered to have been abrogated and superseded by the adherence of Japan to the UCC Geneva, effective April 28, 1956.

[9] Bilateral copyright relations between the People's Republic of China and the United States of America were established,

effective March 17, 1992, by a Presidential Proclamation of the same date, under the authority of section 104 of title 17 of the United States Code, as amended by the Act of Oct. 31, 1988 (Public Law 100-568, 102 Stat. 2853, 2855).

[10] The dates of adherence by Germany to multilateral treaties include adherence by the Federal Republic of Germany when that country was divided into the Federal Republic of Germany and the German Democratic Republic. However, through the accession, effective Oct. 3, 1990, of the German Democratic Republic to the Federal Republic of Germany, in accordance with the German Unification Treaty of Aug.31, 1990, the German Democratic Republic ceased, on the said date, to be a sovereign state. Previously, the German Democratic Republic had become party to the Paris Act of the Berne Convention for the Protection of Literary and Artistic Works on Feb. 18, 1978, but ceased to be a party to the said Convention on Oct. 3, 1990. The German Democratic Republic had also been a member of the Universal Copyright Convention, having become party to the Geneva text of the said Convention on Oct. 5, 1973, and party to the revised Paris text of the same Convention on Dec. 10, 1980.

[11] See also Czech Republic and Slovakia.

[12] Prior to the return of Hong Kong to China, bilateral copyright relations existed with Hong Kong through the United Kingdom (from Aug. 1, 1973), and Phonogram Convention Membership existed through the United Kingdom (from March 4, 1975).

[13] Bilateral copyright relations between the Socialist Republic of Vietnam and the United States were established effective December 23, 1998, by Presidential Proclamation No. 7161 of that same date, at 63 Fed. Reg. 71571 (1998), under the authority of sections 104(b)(5) and 104A(g) of title 17 of the United States Code, as amended.

[14] Bilateral copyright relations between the United States and Belgium, France, the United Kingdom, and Switzerland were established effective July 1, 1891, by Presidential Proclamation No. 3. of that same date, at 27 Stat. 981 (1891), under the authority of The Chase Act of 1891.

[15] Bilateral copyright relations between the United States and Germany were established effective July 12, 1967, by Presidential Proclamation No. 3792 of that same date, at 32 Fed. Reg. 10341, under the authority of Copyright Act of 1909 amended at 55 Stat. 732.

[16] Bilateral copyright relations between Jordan and the United States were established pursuant to the Agreement between the United States of America and the Hashemite Kingdom of Jordan on the Establishment of a Free Trade Area, signed Oct. 24, 2000, and effective Dec. 17, 2001.

[17] Each of the following Commonwealth of Independent States (CIS) countries: Armenia, Azerbaijan, Belarus, Georgia, Kazakhstan, Kyrgyz Republic, Moldova, Russia, Tajikistan, Turkmenistan, Ukraine, and Uzbekistan (but not the CIS countries Latvia, Lithuania, and Estonia) is a successor state to the Soviet Union's copyright treaty obligations, in particular, the obligations under the UCC Geneva, and accordingly is a member of the UCC Geneva effective May 27, 1973, the date the Soviet Union became a party. The successor status in each case was confirmed in a bilateral trade agreement between each of these countries and the United States, effective in each case on the date set forth below. Note that the successor status is consistent with the treatment by UNESCO (secretariat for the UCC) of these countries. The effective dates of the bilateral agreements with the United States confirming the successor status are as follows:

> Azerbaijan (April 21, 1995)
> Belarus (Feb. 16, 1993)
> Georgia (Aug. 13, 1993)
> Kazakhstan (Feb. 18, 1993)
> Kyrgyz Republic (Aug. 21, 1992)
> Moldova (July 2, 1992)
> Russia (June 17, 1992)
> Tajikistan (Nov. 24,1993)
> Turkmenistan (Oct. 25,1993)
> Ukraine (June 23,1992)
> Uzbekistan (Jan. 13, 1994)

Library of Congress • Copyright Office • 101 Independence Avenue, S.E. • Washington, D.C. 20559-6000
www.copyright.gov

August 2003—xxxx Web Rev: August 2003   ♻ Printed on recycled paper   U.S. Government Printing Office: 2003-xxx

© opyright
United States Copyright Office

Copyright Office Fees

In General

The 1976 Copyright Act (title 17 of the *United States Code*) established statutory fees for certain services provided by the Copyright Office. These services include registering claims to copyright and renewal of claims, as well as recording documents, searching copyright records, and other services. In 1997 Congress passed a law giving the Register of Copyrights the authority to set these fees if certain conditions were met. (See Pub. L. 105-80, III Stat. 1529 (1997).) Section 708(b) authorizes the Register of Copyrights to charge fees for other special services. The additional fees are fixed on the "basis of the cost of providing the service … for any other special services requiring a substantial amount of time or expense."

Payment of Fees

All remittances should be in the form of checks, bank money orders, or bank drafts payable to *Register of Copyrights*. Electronic transfers of funds are not accepted except to preregister an unpublished work or to replenish an established Copyright Office deposit account. For information on deposit accounts, request Circular 5, *How to Open and Maintain a Deposit Account in the Copyright Office.*

If a check received in payment of the registration filing fee is returned to the Copyright Office as uncollectible, the Copyright Office will cancel the registration and will notify the remitter. Be advised that it may take a number of weeks before your check is cashed. Please ensure that your account is adequately funded for at least several months.

The registration filing fee for processing an original, supplementary, renewal, or preregistration application is nonrefundable, whether or not copyright registration or preregistration is ultimately made.

Do not send cash. The Copyright Office cannot assume any responsibility for the loss of currency sent in payment of copyright fees.

Foreign Payments

All foreign checks or money orders must be redeemable without a service or exchange fee through a U.S. institution, payable in U.S. dollars, and imprinted with American Banking Association routing numbers. Foreign banks that have affiliates with American financial institutions may be able to provide this service. Postal money orders and international money orders that are negotiable only at a post office are not acceptable.

If you cannot obtain a bank draft as described above, you may either submit signed traveler's checks for the total amount in U.S. dollars; or send your material to a U.S. contact, who may then submit the material with appropriate payment.

© 4.0706

Copyright Office Fee Schedule

Alternatively, if you conduct significant business with our office, you may wish to consider establishing a Deposit Account from which the fees may be paid. See Circular 5 for details.

Certain Fees and Services May Be Charged to a Credit Card

Some fees may be charged by telephone or in person in the office. Others may only be charged in person in the office. Credit card payments are generally authorized only for services that do not require filing of applications or other materials. An exception is made for fees related to items that are hand-delivered to the Public Information Office.

- *Certifications and Documents Section*: Fees for the following services may be charged in person in the office or by phone: additional certificates; copies of documents and deposits; searching, locating, and retrieving deposits; certifications; and expedited processing.

- *Public Information Office*: Fees for the following services may only be charged in person in the office, not by phone: registration forms; special handling requests for all registration requests; special handling requests for services provided by the Certifications and Documents Section; search requests, but only those for which a fee estimate has been provided; additional fee for each claim using the same deposit; full-term retention; request for reconsideration; secure test processing; short fee payments; in-process retrieval; and online service providers.

- *Reference and Bibliography Section*: Requests for search estimates and for searches on a regular or expedited basis may be charged to a credit card by phone.

- *Records Maintenance Unit*: Onsite use of Copyright Office computers, printers, or photocopiers may be charged in person in the office.

- *Fiscal Control Section*: Deposit accounts maintained by the Fiscal Control Section may be replenished by credit card. See Circular 5 for details.

Payment of Fees for Recordation on Form GATT and NIEs

Credit cards may be used for filings under the Uruguay Round Agreements (URAA) when submitted in a timely manner. These filings include requests to record Notices of Intent to Enforce a copyright and claims to copyright made on Form GATT. The Copyright Office will accept Visa, MasterCard, and American Express for these filings. Debit cards cannot be accepted for payment.

To pay by credit card, the filer must provide in a separate letter the credit card's name, number, and expiration date;

the total amount authorized to be charged; and a signature authorizing the Copyright Office to charge the fees to that account. To protect its security, the credit card number must not appear on the NIE or Form GATT because the notice and/or application becomes part of the public record.

Claims filed on Form GATT and requests to record Notices of Intent to Enforce (NIE) may be paid by credit card if the card number is included in a separate letter that accompanies the form or by deposit account. See Circular 5 for details.

Conversion of Checks and Money Orders

Checks and money orders presented in payment for Copyright Office services are converted into an Electronic Funds Transfer (EFT). The Copyright Office will copy your check and use the account information on it to debit your account electronically for the amount of the check. The debit from your account will usually occur within 24 hours after processing and will be shown on your regular account statement.

You will not receive your original check back. The Office will destroy your original check, but will keep an electronic copy of it. If the EFT cannot be processed for technical reasons, the Office will reprocess a printed copy of your original check. If the EFT cannot be completed because of insufficient funds, your service request will not be processed.

Services Provided

Registration of Copyright Claims

The Copyright Office sends a cerificate bearing its official seal for each registration. For further information about copyright registration procedures, request Circular 1, *Copyright Basics*.

Recordation of Documents

A document that relates to any disposition of a copyright, such as a transfer, will, license, or NIE (other than statutory lisence documents) may be recorded in the Copyright Office. The $95 basic fee covers a document of any length containing one title. Additional titles are $25 for each group of 10 or fewer titles. The Copyright Office will verify title counts.

When recordation is completed, the Office will return the submitted document(s) with a certificate of recordation bearing its official seal.

For more information about recordation of documents, request Circular 12, *Recordation of Transfers and Other Documents*. For further information about registering an NIE, including a correction NIE, or registering a restored work under the URAA, request Circular 38B, *Highlights of*

Copyright Office Fee Schedule

Copyright Amendments Contained in the Uruguay Round Agreements Act (URAA).

Certifications

Fees are cumulative. When the Copyright Office certifies a record, a certification fee is payable in addition to fees for other applicable services, such as searches or photoduplication. There is an additional charge of $150 for each hour or fraction of an hour required to locate completed Copyright Office records, except where the requestor supplies the Copyright Office with the registration number and year of registration.

Under certain circumstances, the Copyright Office will locate and retrieve in-process materials for certification or other purposes. The charge to retrieve in-process materials is $150 per hour. For more information about this service, request Circular 6, *Obtaining Access to and Copies of Copyright Office Records and Deposits.*

Anyone may request an additional certificate of registration, copies of the copyright application, correspondence, and other documents related to copyright. These services may be provided under certain conditions on an expedited basis. Copies of the copyright deposit will be provided only when 1) written authorization is received from the copyright claimant of record or his or her designated agent or from the owner of any of the exclusive rights in the copyright; 2) the Copyright Office Litigation Statement Form is completed and received from an attorney in connection with actual or prospective litigation involving the copyrighted work; or 3) a court order is issued for a reproduction of a deposited article, facsimile, or identifying portion that is the subject of litigation in the court's jurisdiction.

Search Reports

A written report is sent for the results of each search made of the Copyright Office's records. Upon request, the Reference and Bibliography Section will estimate the fee required for a search. The fee for a search estimate is $100, which is applicable to the search fee. The hourly search fee is $150. The Office will begin work only after the receipt of the search estimate fee or at least 1 hour's search fee.

NOTE: The Office will not search to determine whether a similar work has already been registered. Such searches are not necessary under the Copyright code.

For more information about this service, request Circular 22, *How to Investigate the Copyright Status of a Work.*

Receipt for Deposits

The certificate of registration will serve as a record of receipt for claims submitted under section 408 of the Copyright Act. For items submitted under section 407 (mandatory deposit for the Library of Congress) the fee for a receipt for deposit is $20.

Special Handling

Expedited processing of an application for registration of a claim to copyright, a mask work claim, a vessel hull design claim, or a request for recordation of documents pertaining to a copyright is granted at the discretion of the Register of Copyrights in certain cases.

Requests must include details that support the basis for the request. Examples of situations where a special handling request may be approved include pending or prospective litigation, cases involving the U.S. Customs Service, contractual matters, or publishing deadlines. The request must include a written certification, that is, a signed statement that the details of the request are correct to the best of the requestor's knowledge.

Requests for special handling should be made in person in the Copyright Public Information Office, 101 Independence Avenue SE, Washington, DC, or by mail to:

Special Handling
Copyright Receiving and Processing
PO Box 71380
Washington, DC 20024-1380

For more information about special handling, request Circular 10, *Special Handling.*

Full-Term Retention of Copyright Deposits

The Copyright Office general policy is to retain published, registered copyright deposits for at least 5 years, with the exception of deposits of published works registered as visual arts. These are retained for at least 10 years. Unpublished deposits, however, are ordinarily kept for the full copyright term. Registrants who wish to ensure that the Copyright Office will keep their published deposits for the full length of the copyright term must pay a fee of $425 to cover processing and storage costs.

Requests for full-term retention should be sent to:

Library of Congress
Copyright Office
Chief, Information and Reference Division
101 Independence Avenue SE
Washington, DC 20559-6000
Attention: Full-Term Retention Request

Copyright Office Fee Schedule

For further information on full-term retention, see "Full-Term Retention of Copyright Deposits" (37 *CFR* 202.23) on the Copyright Office website at *www.copyright.gov/title37/index.html*.

Expedited Reference and Bibliography Searches

This service involves researching Copyright Office records for information on copyright registrations, renewals, transfers and other documents. It may be provided on an expedited basis under certain conditions; call the Reference and Bibliography Section at (202) 707-6850 for more information. The fee for expedited service is $400 per hour or fraction thereof.

Surcharge for Expedited Certifications and Documents Services

The fees for *expedited* services by Certifications and Documents staff are surcharges and will be added to the regular charge for the service or services provided (minimum 1 hour).

Preregistration

Works that are unpublished, are in the process of being prepared for commercial distribution, and fall within certain classes of works are eligible for preregistration. Preregistration takes place electronically on Form PRE, which is available only on the Copyright Office website at *www.copyright.gov*. The fee of $100 must be paid online by deposit account established in the Copyright Office or by credit card, debit card, or electronic funds transfer. For further information, go to the Copyright Office website.

Refunds

Payments more than $50 in excess of the required fee will be refunded automatically, but refunds of $50 or less will only be made upon written request.

Filing fees remitted to the Copyright Office for basic, supplementary or renewal registration, for preregistration, and for special handling will not be refunded, whether or not copyright registration or preregistration is ultimately made. To cover administrative and processing costs, fees received in conjunction with requests for services may not be refunded even when the services cannot be provided.

Before making any refund for fees remitted in relation to nonregistration services, the Copyright Office will deduct an administrative processing fee in an amount equivalent to 1 hour of the requested service, or the minimum fee for the service (37 *CFR* 201.6(c)).

Requests for Reconsideration

When the Copyright Office refuses to register a claim to copyright, it notifies the applicant in writing of the refusal to register. After such notification, the applicant may seek reconsideration not later than 3 months after the date that appears on the Office's written refusal by sending a letter requesting reconsideration and setting forth his or her objections to the refusal. The cost of a first request for reconsideration is $250 plus $25 for each additional claim in a related group. If registration is again refused, a second request for reconsideration may be submitted. The cost of a second reconsideration is $500 plus $25 for each additional claim in a related group. The decision of the Copyright Board of Review for the second request for reconsideration constitutes final agency action.

For Further Information

Information via the Internet

Circulars, announcements, regulations, other related materials, and all copyright application forms are available from the Copyright Office website at *www.copyright.gov*.

Information by telephone

For general information about copyright, call the Copyright Public Information Office at (202) 707-3000. The TTY number is (202) 707-6737. Staff members are on duty from 8:30 AM to 5:00 PM, eastern time, Monday through Friday, except federal holidays. Recorded information is available 24 hours a day. Or, if you know which application forms and information circulars you want, you may request them 24 hours a day from the Forms and Publications Hotline at (202) 707-9100. You may leave a recorded message.

Information by regular mail

Write to:

> *Library of Congress*
> *Copyright Office*
> *Publications Section*
> *101 Independence Avenue SE*
> *Washington, DC 20559-6000*

© Copyright Office Fees

Effective as of July 1, 2006

Basic Registrations

Fee to accompany an application and deposit for registration of a claim to copyright

$45   Form TX, Short Form TX, Form VA, Short Form VA, Form PA, Short Form PA, Form SE, Short Form SE, Form SR, and Form GATT
—   Form GR/CP (*This form is an adjunct to Forms VA, PA, and TX. There is no additional charge.*)

Renewal Registrations

For works published or registered before January 1, 1978

$75   Form RE
$220 Addendum to Form RE

Group Registrations

Fee to register a group of related claims, where appropriate

$25   Form SE/Group (serials) (*per issue, with minimum 2 issues*)
$70   Form G/DN (daily newspapers and newsletters)
$45   Published phographs (*Form VA. Up to 750 published photographs may be identified on form GR/PPh/CON with a single filing fee.*)

Supplementary Registrations

Fee to make a correction or amplification to a completed registration

$115 Form CA
$100 Preregistration

Miscellaneous Registrations

$200 Form D-VH (vessel hulls)
$95   Form MW (mask works)

Special Services Related to Registration (Optional Services)

Special Handling for Registration of Qualified Copyright Claims

Fee to expedite processing of qualified claims

$685 Special handling fee (*per claim*)
$50   Additional fee for each (nonspecial handling) claim using the same deposit

Other Fees Associated with Registration

$425 Full-term retention of published copyright deposit
$150 Secure test processing (*$/hr*)
$45   Handling extra copy for certification

Requests for Reconsideration
(*For claims previously refused registration*)

$250 First request
$25   Additional claim in related group (*each*)
$500 Second request
$25   Additional claim in related group (*each*)

Other Copyright Service Fees

Recordation of Documents Relating to Copyrighted Works

Fee to make a public record of an assignment of rights or other document

$95   Recordation of a document, including a Notice of Intention to Enforce, containing no more than one title
$25   Additional titles (*per group of 10 or fewer titles*)
$435 Special handling of recordation of documents

Reference & Bibliography Reports on Copyrighted Works

Fee for searching copyright records and preparing an official report

$100 Estimate of search fee
$150 Preparation of a report from official records (*$/hr*)
$400 Expedited Reference and Bibliography reports (*$/hr*)

Certification & Documents Services:
Preparing Copies of Copyright Office Records

Fees for locating, retrieving, and reproducing records

$150 Locating and/or retrieving Copyright Office records (*$/hr*)
$40   Additional certificate of registration
$150 Certification of Copyright Office records (*$/hr*)
—   Copying fee: variable depending on format and size
$150 Locating and/or retrieving in-process materials (*$/hr*)
$240 Surcharge for expedited Certification & Documents services listed above or for certification of a Reference & Bibliography search report (*$/hr*)

Miscellaneous Fees

$20   Receipt for deposit without registration (*Section 407 deposit*)
$80   Online Service Provider Designation (Recordation of an Interim Designation of Agent to Receive Notification of Claimed Infringement under §512(c)(2))
$50   Notice to Libraries and Archives (*each additional title: $20*)

Deposit Account Service Charges

$150 Overdraft
$75   Dishonored replenishment check

For Licensing Division fees, request SL-4L.

Copyright Office fees are subject to change. For current fees, check the Copyright Office website at *www.copyright.gov*, write the Copyright Office, or call (202) 707-3000.

Glossary

author Generally a writer, but in the context of the Copyright Act, it includes anyone who creates an original work.

assignment Transfer of copyright ownership from one person or entity to another.

attribution, right of Ensures that artists are properly identified with the works of art they create and that they are not identified with works they did not create.

automated database A body of facts, data, or other information assembled into an organized format suitable for use in a computer and comprising one or more files.

Berne Convention An international copyright treaty that requires all signatories to eliminate formality requirements as a condition to copyright protection. But the formality requirements eliminated by amendment remain important because works created after 1978, the enactment date of the act of 1976, but before 1989, when the act of 1976 was revised and when the United States signed the Berne Convention, are governed by the first version of the 1976 act.

bundle of rights All of the individual rights conferred by copyright, namely, the right to copy, distribute, prepare derivative works, display publicly, and perform publicly.

collective works Defined in the Copyright Act as "a number of contributions, constituting separate and independent works in themselves . . . assembled into a collective whole." Individuals or entities who combine individual contributions into one collection hold the copyright in the collection as a whole. But the individual authors retain rights to their individual works apart from the collection. Thus, other than the rights to reproduce and distribute the collection, and the right to create a derivative work of the collection, the individual contributors to the collection retain the copyright to their individual contributions.

copies According to the Copyright Act, material objects, other than phonorecords, in which a work is fixed by any method now known or later developed, and from which the work can be perceived, reproduced, or otherwise communicated, either directly or with the aid of a machine or device. The term "copies" includes the material object, other than a phonorecord, in which the work is first fixed.

copyleft A play on the word "copyright" used by a few people who have created a movement to oppose what they deem to be an unfair monopoly on creative expression held by copyright owners, particularly in the software industry. This term is not found in the Copyright Act itself. Rather, it was created to challenge established copyright laws. "Copyleft" is used primarily by members of the Free Software Foundation, which promotes GNU, a project designed to provide software that is free from licensing fees or restrictions on use. Richard Stallman started the GNU project in 1983 based on his belief that software should contain a notice and a General Public License that grants reuse and reproduction rights to everyone and requires anyone who uses it to grant the same rights to others.

copyright The exclusive rights of a copyright owner of a work to make and distribute copies, prepare derivative works, and perform and display the work publicly.

copyright registration Submitting the copyrighted work to the Copyright Office, pursuant to the rules and guidelines set forth by that office.

created The fixing of a work in a copy or phonorecord for the first time. When a work is prepared over time, the portion of it that has been fixed at any particular time constitutes the work as of that time; and when the work has been prepared in different versions, each version constitutes a separate work.

damages Generally, a sum of money paid in compensation for loss or injury.

deposit The physical copy or copies that must be submitted to the Copyright Office along with a copyright registration form.

fair use A doctrine that permits use of copyrighted materials for certain purposes listed in the Copyright Act, such as criticism, comment, news reporting, teaching (including multiple copies for classroom use), scholarship, or research. While technically infringing on the copyright owner's rights, these uses are considered permissible; and such fair use can be used as a defense against a claim of copyright infringement.

independent contractor One who is self-employed and has the right to control the means and methods of performing work.

integrity, right of Allows a visual artist to protect his or her work from modifications or destruction that injures the artist's reputation.

joint work A work prepared by two or more authors with the intention that their contributions be merged into inseparable or interdependent parts of a unitary whole.

legal vetting See vetting.

licensing agreement An agreement that sets forth the terms that allow others the limited right to use your work (or for you to use the work of others). You remain the owner of the copyright. A license can be exclusive (only the licensee can use it) or non-exclusive (the licensee can use your work but cannot exclude others from doing so).

literary works Works, other than audiovisual works, expressed in words, numbers, or other verbal or numerical symbols or indicia, regardless of the nature of the material objects, such as books, periodicals, manuscripts, phonorecords, film, tapes, disks, or cards in which they are embodied.

moral rights Refers collectively to the right of attribution and the right of integrity.

orphan works Works that are difficult or impossible to link with their proper owners.

phonorecords Material objects, such as cassette tapes, CDs, or LPs—but not motion picture soundtracks on which sounds are recorded and which combine moving images and sound.

poor man's copyright The myth that if you mail yourself a copy of your work and do not open it, you can use it to establish the date that your work existed in case you ever need to defend your work or challenge a work you believe infringes on your rights. The poor man's copyright does *not* offer any additional protection beyond that which already exists once your idea is fixed and thus your work is created. Additionally it does *not* constitute a registration of your copyright.

privacy, right of The right to be left alone. The three generally recognized invasions of privacy are intrusion, unreasonable publicity, and false light.

publication The distribution of copies or phonorecords of a work to the public by sale or other transfer of ownership, or by rental, lease, or lending. The offering to distribute copies or phonorecords to a group of persons for purposes of further distribution, public performance, or public display constitutes publication. A public performance or display of a work does not of itself constitute publication.

public domain The total absence of copyright protection in a work. A work in the public domain is available to anyone to copy, distribute, perform, display, make derivatives of, or use as he or she sees fit. The author of a work in the public domain has none of the exclusive rights that apply to a copyrighted work. Note that the public domain is not an actual place or database but a term that describes the absence of copyright protection. Furthermore, it does not refer to freeware or shareware. In actuality, free- and shareware are copyrighted software distributed without advance payment.

publicity, right of A person's exclusive right to use his or her name, likeness, or other aspect of his or her persona, and the right to prevent others from using those aspects without authorization.

publisher A person or entity that produces any periodical, magazine, newspaper, book, manual, advertising materials, or other similar material, whether in printed, electronic, or other form.

subsidiary rights Rights that are secondary to the primary publishing right, which is most often the right to publish the manuscript in print form. Subsidiary rights are generally less important (but still valuable) to the publisher, and can include mass market paperback rights, book club rights, and foreign and translation rights; they can also include rights in media other than books, such as motion picture and television rights, stage plays (dramatic rights), electronic rights, performance rights, and more.

vetting A line-by-line review of a manuscript for potential legal issues.

work made for hire A legal doctrine which says that for purposes of copyright protection, the one who commissioned the work to be created by an independent contractor, and not the creator of the work, is the owner of that work; and that an employer owns the copyright to any artistic or literary work that is created by an employee on company time using company equipment.

About the Author

Tonya M. Evans-Walls is the managing attorney of TME Law and practices in the areas of entertainment law (literary, music, and film), intellectual property (copyright and trademark), estate planning, and municipal finance. She is the co-chair of the Pennsylvania Bar Association Sports, Entertainment, and Art Law committee, and is a nationally recognized speaker on publishing and intellectual property law and estate planning issues. Evans-Walls is an adjunct professor at York College of Pennsylvania and teaches a course on entertainment law.

Evans-Walls is also a poet and the author of numerous books, including *Literary Law Guide for Authors: Copyright, Trademark, and Contracts in Plain Language*; *Copyright Companion for Writers*; *Contracts Companion for Writers*; *Seasons of Her: A Collection of Poetry*; and *SHINE!* Her short story, *Not Tonight*, appears in an anthology titled *Proverbs for the People*, published by Kensington. Forthcoming books include *And Then One Day She Knew*, *The Blues*, and *An Old Soul Reborn*.

Evans-Walls attended Northwestern University on a tennis scholarship and graduated on the Dean's List. She received an academic scholarship to attend Howard University School of Law; she served as editor-in-chief of the *Howard Law Journal* and graduated with honors.

Prior to attending law school, Evans-Walls competed on the women's professional tennis circuit and played most notably in the US Open, Virginia Slims of Philadelphia, and Lipton in 1993. She lives in Philadelphia with her husband, O. Russel Walls, III, and is a member of Alpha Kappa Alpha Sorority.

Acknowledgments

First, I give honor to God for blessing me with the gift of writing and teaching, and for making ways out of no way and opening windows whenever a door closes.

I acknowledge and thank my amazing husband and perfect provision, Russel, for supporting my every endeavor and for granting me the necessary quiet time and space to complete this project. Thanks for the wonderful meals, great wine, and my Oolong and Chai tea even before I asked, whenever it looked as if I needed a boost or a little encouragement. And thank you for not freaking out when you awoke to find me asleep on the couch surrounded by my laptop, printouts, and several (yes, at least three) tea cups, when we both know I only need one!

With deep appreciation I thank my outstanding editor, Lisa A. Smith, who always goes above and beyond the call of duty in her efforts to make a good book great and is second to none in her editing skills. Lisa is the best editor and project manager I've *never* seen. We will have to stop *not* meeting like this!

Many thanks to Dan Poynter for continuing to assist me—and countless other writers—to home in on my vision to write and publish with excellence and for nourishing the seedling of a great idea to its fruition as a complete line of legal reference guides for writers. Dan, you are a true trailblazer and a man who not only talks the talk but walks the walk.

I sincerely appreciate the fine efforts of the other professionals who participated in this project, namely, James "True" Jones for cover design, Pam Rider for her indexing services, and Deb Tremper for her wonderful interior design work to bring this subject matter to life visually.

Index

Books Published By Legal Write Publications

Literary Law Guide for Authors: Copyright, Trademark, and Contracts in Plain Language

Copyright Companion for Writers

Contracts Companion for Writers

E-Books for Writers

9 Things Every Writer MUST Know about the Law

Writing about Real People and Places:
    How to Successfully Navigate the Rights of Publicity and Privacy

Using Other People's Words: Fair Use, Permissions, and Work Made for Hire

International Copyright Issues

What Every Freelancer Should Know about Copyright

What Every Songwriter Should Know about Copyright

Other Services

Lit Law for Writers on the GO! Podcast at www.literarylawguide.com

Lit Law for Writers on the GO! Blog at litlawblog.blogspot.com

If you have a topic you'd like to see covered in a future edition, e-mail your question, comment, or topic to info@literarylawguide.com, or visit www.literarylawguide.com.

Notes

Notes

Notes

Direct Sales Order Form

For info: info@legalwritepublications.com

Web orders: www.legalwritepublications.com

Fax orders: 215-438-0469. Send this form.

Phone orders: 215-438-0468. Have your credit card ready.

Mail orders: Order Fulfillment, P.O. Box 25216, Philadelphia, PA, 19119 USA

Bulk orders: info@legalwritepublications.com for discounts and specials for clubs, schools, and organizations

Trade orders: Trade orders handled by Independent Publishers Group

    Phone: 800-888-4741

    E-mail: orders@ipgbook.com

    Mail: Independent Publishers Group
             Order Department
             814 North Franklin Street
             Chicago, IL 60610

    Web: www.ipgbook.com

Titles ordered

Title	Quantity
Title	Quantity
Title	Quantity

Please send me information on: *(check all that apply)*

❏ Other books   ❏ Speaking/Seminars/Events/Performances   ❏ E-newsletter   ❏ Legal services

Please print clearly.

Name

Address

City   State   Zip

Phone   E-mail

Sales tax: Please add 6% for products shipped to Pennsylvania addresses outside of Philadelphia and 7% for Philadelphia addresses.

Shipping: $4.55 US for the first book, $2.00 US for each additional book. International $15.00 US for the first book, $5 US for each additional book.

Payment: ❏ Check   ❏ Visa   ❏ MasterCard   ❏ Am Ex

Card number   Exp   Name on card

Billing Address (if different from above)